SELF-DEVELOPMENT FOR SUCCESS

Effective interviews

Acknowledgements

A great deal of what I know about looking for jobs and being interviewed has been learnt with and from my clients at Management Futures, the consultancy which I started when I, too, was in career-change mode. I would like to thank the clients who have enabled me to learn such a lot from them, whether it has been from the recruitment side as employers, or as individuals seeking help with the exciting and often daunting process of changing jobs.

I also particularly thank Jan Campbell of Dearden Management, Director of the NHS Career Service, Executive Choice, for the fun and challenge of involving me in a project which continues to enrich my experience. All of the books mentioned in the reading list have proved useful and practical, but I especially acknowledge a debt to Richard Bolles for his superb, annually-produced and ever-friendly guide to the whole process of finding a new job.

SELF - DEVELOPMENT FOR SUCCESS

Effective interviews

THE ESSENTIAL GUIDE TO THINKING AND WORKING SMARTER

Jenny Rogers

AMERICAN MANAGEMENT ASSOCIATION

AMACOM
American Management Association
New York • Atlanta • Boston • Chicago • Kansas City
San Francisco • Washington, D. C.
Brussels • Mexico City • Tokyo • Toronto

A Marshall Edition
Conceived, edited, and designed by
Marshall Editions Ltd.
The Orangery, 161 New Bond Street
London W1Y 9PA

This book is available at a special discount when ordered in bulk quantities. For information, contact Special Sales Department, AMACOM, an imprint of AMA Publications, a division of American Management Association,1601 Broadway, New York, NY 10019.

This publication is designed to provide accurate and authoritative information in regard to the subject matter covered. It is sold with the understanding that the publisher is not engaged in rendering legal, accounting, or other professional service. If legal advice or other expert assistance is required, the services of a competent professional person should be sought.

Library of Congress Cataloging-in-Publication Data
Rogers, Jennifer.
    Effective interviews / Jenny Rogers.
        p.   cm.
    Includes biographical references and index.
    ISBN 0-8144-7021-1
    1. Emplyment interviewing.   I Title.
HF5549.5.I6R643 1999
650.14--dc21   98-53809
                                                              CIP

Printing number

10 9 8 7 6 5 4 3 2 1

Consultant Editor Chris Roebuck
Project Editor Conor Kilgallon
Design Strukture Design
Art Director Sean Keogh
Managing Editor Clare Currie
Editorial Assistant Sophie Sandy
Editorial Coordinator Rebecca Clunes
Production Nikki Ingram

Cover photography The Image Bank

Originated in Italy by Articolor
Printed and bound in Portugal by Printer Portuguesa

Contents

Chapter 1
Introduction   8
The work context   9
10 golden tips for getting the job   11
The other side: how interviewers
approach their task   14

Chapter 2
Researching the organization   18
Being the solution to the employer's
problems   22
Your USP   24
Your USP: some examples   26
Self-presentation   28
Mental preparation   30

Chapter 3
Confirmation of date and time   34
Getting there   35
The interview as a two-way process   36
The interview as a social event   39
Interview questions   42
Giving, not taking   43
Using the evidence-based technique   44
Things never to say or do at an
interview   46
Coping with incompetent interviewers   49
Awkward questions: some answers   55
Asking your own questions   58
On-the-spot hire   60
Assessment centers   62
Behaviour that helps at Assessment
Centres   68

Giving a presentation   70
Keeping in touch with the audience   74
'Trial by orange juice'   76
The practice interview   78

Chapter 4
If you don't get the job   82
The follow-up letter   84
Do I really want the job?   86
Starting the job   91

Index   94
Further reading   95

1

**Introduction
Tips for success
The interviewer's approach**

The work context

The selection lottery

Unspoken questions

Introduction

The book aims to show you how to prepare effectively for a job interview including overcoming 'nerves'. There is a section on handling even the most difficult questions during the interview. The book also uncovers the secrets of Assessment Centers, the seemingly mysterious process where you might be asked to undergo psychological tests or take part in a discussion with other candidates. These are still comparatively rare situations, but more and more organizations are approaching selection in this way, so it is a good idea to be prepared.

The activity does not end with the offer of a job because then there is the problem of negotiating a salary and settling into the new position effectively.

A daunting task

Getting through a job interview is definitely one of life's scarier hurdles. The whole process can re-awaken some of our most primitive fears. You may approach every interview with dread, fearing rejection. If you are a modest and unassuming person, you may hate feeling that you have to perform in order to get hired. The idea of being judged not good enough on the basis of a few hours of contact can also create strong feelings of anger over the unfairness of it all.

You should read this book if you:

- **Are getting interviews but not getting the job.**
- **Have been laid off from your present job and are looking for another.**
- **Are returning to work after a career break or illness.**
- **Are an internal candidate for a job that you know will be coming up soon.**
- **Are simply restless and know that you will be looking for a new job in the near future.**

Then, of course, there are the implications of actually getting the job, which can mean relocating to another city, changing the children's schools, and disrupting a spouse or partner's career as well.

At the same time, getting a new job can be the gateway to renewed self-esteem, more money, and more fulfillment. It is truly exasperating to fail to land a job that you know you could have done well.

This book takes the mystery out of the job interview. Reading it and practicing the techniques it advises will definitely increase your chances of getting the job you want – and deserve!

The work context

Why personnel can be hard to find

Organizations repeatedly complain that they cannot recruit suitable people. They say that there are acute skill shortages. My company's experience certainly shows this to be true. For instance, in the last few years I have been involved in the following:

- Helping a charity to select a chief executive and finding that in spite of their assembling what looked like a decent short list, it was not possible to make an appointment. All the candidates appeared to be unsuitable in one way or another.

- The selection of another senior person for a well-known non-profit organization. A candidate was chosen, but turned the job down in favor of one at a much higher salary for another organization. This candidate, by the way, was well into his fifties, thus giving the lie to the idea that getting past a certain age (35, 40, 50… all have been cited as "too old") disqualifies you from a job.

- Being approached by an employer to help them re-craft their job specification (the template for all recruitment) because they wanted to recruit someone for a very senior role, and had been unable even to assemble a short list of suitable candidates, in spite of trying to do so for some months.

- Working with an employer who had twice spent a very large sum of money on advertising in the *Wall Street Journal,* and yet had been unable to recruit the person they wanted – a vacancy that was eventually filled by executive search ("head-hunting").

Yet in spite of this, we all know that unemployment remains a reality in today's job market. Whether the business cycle is on the upswing or downswing, companies still engage in periodic "downsizing" and thus eliminate various types of jobs. What is going on here?

The most important reason is the nature of work has changed permanently. The days when a job could be defined for some years by a standard job description have gone for good. This is because of the huge changes that have swept the global economy over the last few years.

The work context

This is too complex an issue to discuss here, but it basically means that when employers do want to appoint, they are increasingly looking for someone special and finding that competition for such people is acute. It can be summed up in the table below:

Whatever your profession or specialty, the qualities on the left are the ones that employers are seeking.

In the interview, you need to demonstrate that you are the kind of person who has these qualities. That is what this book is about.

Employers want people who can	Avoid people who
Solve problems	Create problems
Work as a team member	Can only work solo
Work as a team leader	Avoid responsibility
Show initiative	Want to be told what to do
Meet tight deadlines	Miss deadlines
Deliver on promises	Over-promise and under-perform
Stay committed to continuous learning	Think their original qualifications are still all that is necessary to do the job
Follow protocols where necessary	Ignore protocols, even when they matter e.g. on health and safety
Influence others skilfully; handle conflict	Get offended easily; run away from conflict
Put customers first	Put customers down
Handle change	Think the good old days were best
Keep positive and enthusiastic, even when the going gets rough	Moan and whine
Stay flexible	Say: "It's not in my job description."

10 golden tips for getting the job

This book will expand on all of these, but essentially there are 10 golden tips:

1 Research the job, the organization (or department, unit)

2 Prepare yourself by having at least one practice interview which anticipates all the obvious questions

3 Wear appropriate dress

4 The interview is a social occasion – handle it so that you make the interviewers feel comfortable

5 Handle all questions by offering evidence of how your experience fits the job

6 Keep your answers to no more than 2-3 minutes

7 The interview is a two-way process; use it to get more information and to decide whether you still want the job

8 Assuming you want the job, convey enthusiasm for it

9 Don't negotiate salary and conditions at the interview – keep it for later when you have actually been offered the job

10 Write a thank you letter after the interview – even if you don't get the job

The selection lottery

Selection is an anxious and exciting time for both interviewee and interviewer. Both sides have a common interest. The employer wants – often desperately – to fill the vacancy. As the interviewee, you have committed yourself this far – to the tedium of crafting your Curriculum Vitae (CV) or application form and to the taxing process of the interview. You may be as eager to get the job as the employer is to fill it.

An interview is not necessarily the best way to find the right person. For instance, research repeatedly shows that the panel interview is a very poor method of selecting staff.

In fact some research shows that it is not much better than hand-writing analysis as a predictor of future performance in the job. There is even some research which suggests that picking candidates with a pin (i.e. completely at random) is just as effective.

10 golden tips for getting the job

You don't have to be an occupational psychologist to see why this might be:

■ Interviewers often use the interview to confirm the negative impressions they form in the first few seconds of meeting you and vice versa.

■ Many interviewers are vain. They believe they have powers of divination. One of my colleagues once overheard a senior personnel professional saying with absolute conviction that he could tell within two minutes whether people were, as he said, "40 watt or 200 watt people." Naturally, he believed he was infallibly choosing the 200 watt people, even though the very high turnover in his unit suggested that something was going wrong with the selection process.

■ Few interviewers have had training in selection skills. Many make appallingly elementary mistakes in the way they interview.

■ Candidates may approach the interview without preparation.

■ Candidates often make the mistake of assuming that their qualities and experience will speak for themselves, thus under-estimating the importance of the interview itself.

■ Interviewers are often nervous and do not listen properly to the answers to their questions.

■ Candidates are often so nervous that they do not do themselves justice.

This combination of interviewer incompetence and candidate innocence can all too often end in a mutually unsatisfactory way. The employer misses the best candidate and the best candidate misses the job.

The interview is still the main method of hiring people. More often than not, it is the only method the employer knows. Even getting references is an increasingly unimportant part of the process. Former bosses may be afraid of being sued if they write critical or uncomplimentary things about a candidate. They now often refuse to do more than confirm job title, duties, salary, and length of service. Perhaps this is just as well, since many references, when they are written, are bland and flavorless.

There are many ways of selecting people which do not have the disadvantages of the interview. However, all take more time and may involve more expense.

Many employers have no experience or even familiarity with these more elaborate processes and thus must rely solely on the personal interview as a selection tool.

Personal experience of bad interview practices include:

- The interview being shamelessly interrupted by an associate of the Great Man carrying out the interview. The associate rushed in to give him the latest prices in his stock portfolio and to ask for buying/selling decisions – which were duly given.

- Being asked about experience of writing and editing when the CV had an attachment listing about 50 books as writer or editor (a good reminder never to rely on the panel having actually read your CV or application form).

- Being the chosen candidate of the panel but not getting the job because it had already been offered before the interviews took place to an old college friend of the Chief Executive.

- The agreed best candidate not getting the job because the panel thought that as a youngish woman, she would not be able to manage a largely middle-aged male group. In this case the vacancy went unfilled.

- A member of the panel falling asleep during the interview.

- A member of the panel leaving with no explanation half way through the interview.

- Having an interview during a winter power outage in a cold and rapidly darkening room where the panel all had their coats on to keep warm.

The other side: how interviewers approach their task

Shocking as it may seem, you should also bear in mind that you cannot rely on all members of the panel having read and properly considered your CV or application form. It is much safer to assume that no one will have read it as carefully as you have written it, even though all panel members will probably have read some bits of it attentively. The shortlisting will probably have been done by no more than two of the panel. Sometimes only the prospective supervisor has been involved. Other panel members may have relied on reading the paperwork while commuting to work or during some free time before the interviews start, or even while the interview is going on.

When you are a candidate, it is difficult to see how things look from the other side of the table. To do a good interview, it helps to know how the interviewers typically approach their task.

The first thing to remember is that at least some of the panel may be feeling nervous. There can be a number of reasons for this. If it is their first time as interviewers, they may be afraid of looking silly in front of colleagues by asking "stupid" questions. What constitutes a "stupid" question may vary according to the organization. In a male-oriented culture, the first-time interviewer may fear being seen as "too soft"; in a gentler culture there may be a fear of looking aggressive and unfriendly. In an organization which prides itself on its intellectual capability, there may be pressure to ask clever rather than wise questions.

More commonly, most interviewers are apprehensive about appointing the wrong person. The costs of making a selection mistake are high. The visible costs include: paying off the person; possibly having to pay for extra help in tandem; re-advertising. The hidden costs include: the time involved in going through the selection process all over again; lost business opportunities; damage to the employer's reputation; loss of direction; and loss of morale – and so on.

Many employers do take a professional approach to selection and know how easily the wrong person can be chosen. Thus the unspoken questions will always be:

■ Have we really found the best person, or if we looked harder, longer, somewhere else, would we find our ideal?

■ How can we find out everything we need to know about the person? What skeletons may be lurking in the closet here?

■ What can this person do for the organization? (Not, as many job-hunters naively think, "what can the organization do for him or her?")

■ Why is he or she looking for a job? And why here?

All of this is why part of your job at the interview is to reassure the panel that:

■ **You are the best person.**
■ **There are no skeletons in your closet.**
■ **You have a lot to offer.**
■ **Your reasons for seeking a job are completely respectable.**

Being sold the job

Note that these points apply even when there are no embarrassing episodes in your employment history.

The other point to remember is that the employer is usually well aware of the need to sell the organization to you. The ideal candidate often seems exasperatingly elusive. When employers think they might have found this ideal, their main worry is "how can we persuade him/her to join us?" All employers are well aware of the imperfections of the organization and will know that whatever the attractive aspects of the job, it will also have its boring and tedious side. They will be careful not to discourage you by mentioning any of this. To find out, you will need to do thorough research of your own.

Interviewing is tiring. To do it properly needs high-level concentration and sustained energy. Many employers pack too many interviews into the day because they want to hedge their bets ("Why don't we see this extra person – he/she might just be the one we want…").

The combination of too many candidates and running too long can mean no breaks and exhausted interviewers.

Finally, there are the panel members who are supremely unconcerned about the importance of the day. They know nothing of questioning technique, the law, or professional selection methods but are perfectly happy to back hunches based on "intuition." This is the I-didn't-get-where-I-am-today-by-being-trained… school of thought. Like the "political" panel member, this person may only give sporadic attention to the process.

There are several clear messages in all of this for you as the candidate. A main part of your job in the interview is:

- **Holding the attention of the entire panel, not just the person who is asking that question. You do this by constantly scanning the group and making brief eye-contact with all of them.**
- **Smiling and looking lively in a way that feels natural to you.**
- **Remembering that the interview is a social occasion, so the talking and replying should be evenly shared between you and the panel.**

When faced with a very large panel – perhaps 10 people, you have to assume that at least half will be there for political reasons only. Their commitment to the process may therefore be questionable, and they may feel it is perfectly all right to daydream their way through the event.

When you arrive for your interview, you are probably, at least, keyed up, at most, tense. It may be hard for you to appreciate that by the time it's your turn, the panel's energy could be flagging.

2

The importance of research
Your USP
Preparing yourself mentally

Useful questions

Solving employer's problems

Presenting yourself

Researching the organization

Approaches to research

You need to adopt a variety of approaches to do this essential work. Where you don't know the organization, you could try:

- Library research, including newspaper clippings. Try the local newspaper if all else fails.

- Calling the public relations department (if the organization is large enough) and asking for the annual report or any other documentation which will tell you something about the organization.

- Any major reports about the organization or its field.

An interviewer once saw 27 candidates over four days of preliminary interviews to fill three posts as a trainee Assistant Producer in a large department at a major television network. The jobs were specially designed for young people already on the staff, but who had not yet made the transition to an editorial post. Of the 27 candidates for this coveted opportunity:

- Six could not name more than one program in the department's lineup.
- Four could name two or three programs, but had not watched any of the lineup.

- Ten had watched one or two programs but only in the week prior to the interview.

- Only four had bothered to visit the department, borrow videos and talk to producers already there.

Two out of the four who had taken the most trouble were among the trio who eventually got the jobs. In another organization, the company was recruiting a legal expert. The first question asked by one candidate was "what does this organization actually do?" He didn't get the job.

Talking to current employees

Talking to people already in the organization, preferably on-site, is always useful. Bear in mind that you need to be tactful: some of the obvious people to approach may also be candidates, or panel members, in which case talking to them is inappropriate.

Where the company is new or small, it is vital to do some research into its stability and financial health. You can look up director's names, profit, etc. in a Standard & Poor's index or a Dun and Bradstreet report.

Useful questions to ask are:

- What's going well in this organization/department/unit?
- What's not going so well?
- What are the "big issues" here and what are the main challenges that lie ahead?
- What would be the ideal solution to these challenges? What's preventing the ideal solution from happening?
- What would need to happen for the ideal to become reality?
- In what direction is this organization/department/unit going?
- Where do you think it is in relation to its competitors? (Even internal departments usually have competitors.)
- What's the main reason for making this appointment?

You should note that these are the questions to ask whatever the level of seniority of the job being offered.

Questions to think about here are:

- Is the company in a healthy financial state?
- What market share does it have?
- What kind of market is it in – is it a stable market or is it an immature market which is also volatile?

Another useful question is to ask about staff turnover. A high staff turnover usually indicates an unhappy team, or else a boss who does not know how to pick people. You will need a certain amount of caution in interpreting this information. Sometimes a high turnover simply indicates that the company has purposely attracted a lot of young people, knowing that they can and must move on quickly.

Researching the organization

Researching the job

Again, a variety of approaches is best. For an existing job, it is always a good idea to talk to the departing job-holder if you can contact them. It makes no difference whether this person is leaving in good or bad odor – they can give you direct information about what is involved in the job, what your potential future boss is like and so on. Where someone has left in a burst of anger, you will naturally need to regard what they say with caution and interpret it judiciously.

Where the job is a non-specialized one and done by a number of people, look for someone who can tell you what it is like on a daily basis. What skills does it need? What are the highs and lows? What's the most taxing single thing they've had to deal with in the last few weeks or months?

Think carefully about recent trends in this job and discuss it with someone already in the field. What reports, articles, legislation, or books will you be expected to know about? Read them, even if it is only a cursory look.

If a named person is quoted in the advertisement, you must contact them: their role is to help you. Not to do so will imply lack of commitment. Such research is bound to be superficial compared with what you learn about an organization once you are inside it. No matter – some research is still vital.

Researching membership of the panel

There should be no mystery about who is going to sit on the panel: it is not a state secret. Contact whoever has invited you to the interview and ask how the panel is to be constituted. This may allow you to anticipate particular questions. For instance, if you know that a senior manager from an internal client department is going to be present, you could reasonably anticipate questions about some aspect of client service.

Identifying what the employer wants

Most employers now send out some helpful documentation in advance of the interview. You will have used this to craft your written application, but it is worth having another look at it before the interview.

The information from the employer may have included any of the following:

■ A person specification, which identifies the "ideal" candidate in terms of experience, education, qualifications, motivation, etc.

■ A job description, which sets out who the person reports to and what the jobholder is responsible for. Many job descriptions are far too long and are often out of date the moment they are written. Some are inflated so as to increase the job-holder's grade according to certain pseudo-scientific, job-analysis systems. Some job descriptions are really just lists of duties, but this is still useful information about what is expected.

■ A competency analysis, which sets out what behavior you would see in a person who was excellent in every aspect of the job. An example would be "customer focus," meaning sensitivity and responsiveness to the needs of customers. Where there is a competency analysis, this is the most important piece of documentation as it shows you that the employer has taken the task of recruiting seriously; it also tells you what skills and qualities the employer is looking for. In an organization that knows how to recruit, the interview will be structured entirely around these competencies and you will be asked for evidence about how your experience fits them.

Study any or all of this carefully, take it apart, and ask yourself:

■ **What skills is the employer looking for?**
■ **What type of person?**
■ **What experience?**

How does your experience match? (Note that all experience is relevant, whether it is professional or obtained in some other setting). For instance, if "customer focus" is one of the competencies the employer wants, what experience will you be able to quote at the interview which will prove that you can look after customers?

Being the solution to the employer's problems

The main point of all this preparation can be reduced to one simple formula. When you are being interviewed or assessed, your main task is to show the employer that you are the solution to their problems. You can only do this if you have a really clear grasp of what the employer's problems are. Here are some examples:

Barbara was initially trained as a nurse and had been laid off from her job as a unit manager at a teaching hospital, which had recently merged with a competitor. She was shortlisted at a hospital that was likewise undergoing staffing changes due to managed care consolidations.

She availed herself of all opportunities to find out what the potential new employer wanted. She talked to the Director of Nursing, visited the hospital and made sure that she talked to six or seven of the staff – including lower level staff as well as senior people, including the Chief Executive. The hospital had recently been the subject of a state Department of Health inquiry, and she obtained a copy of the final report off the Internet and studied it carefully.

From all of this research she concluded that:

■ Morale was low and the main task of any newly appointed manager would be to build morale among managerial and clinical staff.

■ There were serious issues surrounding quality of patient care which needed to be addressed.

■ There was still a great deal of public disquiet about the hospital with a hostile local media.

■ Anyone in a senior job in the trust would have to be responsible for some of the public relations.

■ More change was inevitable and any new manager would have to be adept at managing it.

In her interview, Barbara emphazised her understanding of the problems the hospital faced, and stressed the relevance of her own experience. She talked about how she had developed the clinical expertise and public relations savvy of her previous team; she described her practical approach to raising standards of care. She talked about the inevitability of more change and built on her experience in her previous post to set out her own approach. She told the interviewing panel about how she was trained to do radio and TV interviews giving her the confidence to handle the media.

Barbara got the job, and was told by the Chief Executive told her that she had 'aced' the interview, despite a really strong shortlist.

Chris is a facilities manager, managing buildings for large employers. Having been in his post for five years at a Fortune 100 company, he wanted to move on. He was approached by a smaller firm that specialized in managing services on a contracted-out basis. They were looking for a senior person to develop new services and make their solicitations more credible.

He spent two days with the firm, and was invited to talk to whoever he wished, so with their encouragement, he called several of their existing clients, asking questions such as: "What do you think of the service now?" and "What circumstances would make you switch to another supplier?"

When Chris returned to the firm to be interviewed, he was able to pinpoint exactly where he felt the job should develop. He offered his views tentatively, but it was clear to the employer that they were based on intelligent research. He stressed how much his present job equipped him to do all of this, and also the value of his experience as a client. Chris got the job.

A note of warning: generally there is everything to be said for this type of research. However, beware of believing that because you have been thorough, you really know all about the organization. If you think this, you may come across as arrogant as well as ignorant. Take this into account, and preface your analysis in the interview with comments like "it seemed from the research I was able to do..." You should also distinguish facts from opinions and quote sources for your views where you can without betraying confidentiality.

In summary, getting the job starts with the preparation you do on the organization.

- It is essential to research the job and the organization because it demonstrates your commitment to the idea of getting the job.
- It helps to decide whether you want to pursue the application. You may uncover things about the job or organization that indicate it is not the place for you. Alternatively, the research may increase your enthusiasm.
- It enables you to make a more convincing application because you are better informed about what the employer wants at the interview.

- You can answer questions in greater depth.
- It will make you stand out among other candidates.
- It shows initiative.

The first and last two points are particularly important. During the interview, employers are searching continuously for evidence that you are their kind of person. All employers want commitment, and 99 percent also want initiative.

Your USP

Finally, you should prepare about five-minutes-worth of material which contains your Unique Selling Proposition (USP). This is a piece of jargon from the world of selling. The product you are selling here is yourself. If you are well interviewed, this will emerge anyway. If you are not, or if the interview takes a turn that leaves out the aspect that you think makes you the strongest bet, then it is vital to have this prepared.

Some examples:

Jason was on the shortlist for a job as a management training consultant and knew that he was one of six strong candidates. His experience included equal time spent as an operations manager and as a trainer. He guessed, rightly, that this would be unusual, since the majority of trainers have become trainers early in their careers and often have little managerial experience. His USP was to say that he understood the issues that participants at his courses faced, as he had been on the front lines himself. Furthermore, he said that this experience gave him credibility with participants. He also had an unusually broad portfolio of training specialties and made sure that he mentioned these in a way that would appeal to the hiring organization by suggesting that these specialties would enable it to increase its product range.

Justine was a social worker assigned to a cancer unit at a children's hospital, and hoped to move into a more visible position involving hospital-patient-family relations. Her USP was to set out the high store she put on interpersonal skills with patients and their families, all of whom would be under great stress. She wanted to make sure that the panel knew what had been achieved by the series of information leaflets she had personally developed, as well as the patient hot-line she had established. One final piece of USP was that her ethnic background gave her a unique cultural and practical insight into the needs of the local minority population.

Diane was a finance specialist for a small firm and was being interviewed for a similar job at a considerably higher salary in a much larger organization. She felt that her USP was the flexibility and the all-round experience that her previous job had given her. Far from it having been a disadvantage to have worked in a small company, Diane was eager to tell the panel that it was a huge plus – she had seen every aspect of the company's performance, and it had taught her where it was important to have effective controls and where it was important to keep a loose rein. She also wanted to emphasize that she was enthusiastic about taking on more responsibility and saw this as an enjoyable challenge.

This process can work very well, even when all seems lost:

Bob had been obliged to tender his resignation in the state Public Works Department after the unit he was managing was pilloried in the press for cost-overruns and incompetence. An administrative aide had made it clear to Bob in private conversation that he had to be the scapegoat, even though his own personal honesty was never in question and an inquiry subsequently exonerated his unit. Before the interview for his new job, Bob was determined to bring this up, even though he felt that the panel might be too embarrassed to ask about it. He wanted to raise it because he felt that the whole experience had taught him a lot about the realities of managing in the public sector. He wanted to say, too, that he was proud of his government service and his unit's accomplishments and felt that its unsung achievements had depended on team work and effective leadership from him and that these were qualities he was eager to bring to the job being advertised.

Finding your USP. Ask yourself these questions:

- From my research, what suggests I am compatible with what this employer wants?
- What problems can I be confident of solving for this employer?
- What am I really good at – what can I do well without even trying?
- What do people consistently praise about my work?
- What are my main achievements – the ones I am really proud of?
- What's unusual about me – for instance some special skill, experience or character?
- How could all of this benefit my future employer?

One important point here is to remember to distinguish features from benefits when you are setting out your USP. A feature is a straight factual statement, whereas a benefit shows how and why it will be a good thing for the other person to "buy". For example, it may be a feature of your career that you have a particular qualification. A benefit of the qualification may be that you have in-depth expertise in an area in which the employer is active – you could use your specialist knowledge to improve the company's performance in that field.

Your USP: some examples

Here are some more examples:

Feature:	Benefit:
I was a project management engineer for two years.	My two years of experience has given me hands-on understanding of engineering project-management, so in this job I would know all the places where cost and time can be saved through careful planning.
I am responsible for new-product development using high-tech methods.	Being responsible for product development means that I could bring you cost-saving expertise in the latest high-tech methods.
I can use "Word" – I'm computer literate.	I do all my own word-processing so I only need modest secretarial support.
I've been responsible for a lot of innovation in my current job.	My track record of innovation in my current job means that you can expect to get a lot of new projects and ideas from me.

What will your USPs be? Use this space to jot down some ideas:

_____

_____

_____

_____

_____

_____

Important uses

The USP is especially important for the interview that is clumsily conducted. This may include rambling interviewers, interview panels who still believe in the "model answer approach" and so on. When you have prepared your USP you are in a much better position to overcome the disadvantages of this kind of interview.

Research checklist:		
Have you:	**Yes**	**No**
Obtained and carefully read the annual report and any other published documents about the organization?		
Visited the organization to see for yourself what it is like?		
Talked to a variety of people in the organization about its major issues?		
Talked to the person who recently did the job, if it is an existing job?		
Talked to other people who do the job, if it is the sort of role filled by several people?		
Found out who will be on the panel?		
Identified what skills the employer is looking for?		
Identified what major problems the appointee will be expected to solve?		
Prepared your USP?		

Self-presentation

This is part of your preparation and should not be left until the last minute, as you may need to get your interview clothes dry-cleaned, your hair cut and so on.

However absurd it seems, the interviewing panel is affected by your appearance. Of course you should not judge a book by its cover, but the panel can only go on the evidence in front of them, and that includes how you look. Interview panels inevitably jump to conclusions, such as:

- She looks impressive – she would do well with our committees.
- She seems like one of us – the staff would like her.
- This person has dirty shoes – this probably means he has a sloppy attitude to work.
- This person looks "unpolished" – she might embarrass us with clients.

The point about self-presentation is that employers are looking for reasons to screen you out, not to count you in, so at the interview you want to minimize the chances of being excluded before you have even spoken.

Dressing for interviews: some basic rules for both sexes

- More formal is always safer than less formal; a smart well-pressed suit in a neutral color is usually the best choice. Never risk anything that could be perceived as vulgar. Don't be fooled by the apparently informal everyday appearance of staff in many organizations. Even here, it is often obligatory to wear formal clothing for an interview.

- Impeccable cleanliness and tidiness is essential: nails, clothing, shoes, hair, body. Make sure your clothes are clean and that you have had a bath or shower and washed your hair. This may seem like insultingly obvious advice, but unfortunately, experience suggests that it is ignored by many candidates. Interview rooms are often small and stuffy, and I have sat in many where the combination of candidate nervousness and unwashed body/stale-smelling clothing has ruled out candidates who otherwise had something good to offer.

This means AVOIDING

For men	For women
Straggly beards (a neatly trimmed beard is fine)	Extremes of hair fashion
Untidy or dirty hair	Untidy or dirty hair
Body odor	Body odor
Smelling of alcohol, or last night's meal	Smelling of alcohol, or last night's meal
Aftershave	Perfume – even the most discreet could seem over-powering; (perfume is also an intensely personal choice and yours may not be shared by the interviewers)
Tobacco odor or stained fingers	Tobacco odor or stained fingers
Jeans, casual clothing, pens in a shirt or jacket pocket	Jeans and casual clothing
Metal badges	
Pointy or high-heeled shoes; boots or sandals	Very high-heeled shoes or clogs; boots
	Bare legs, sandals; brightly-colored shoes and handbags
Tight clothing	Lots of cleavage, no bra, tight clothing, very short skirts, anything see-through
Jewelry other than a watch or wedding ring	Lots of jewelry especially if it makes a noise; charm bracelets; dangling earrings; ankle bracelets
Joke socks	
Joke ties	
Extremes of fashion	Extremes of fashion
Over-bright colors	
Crumpled clothing	Wrinkled or unpressed clothing

Mental preparation

Calming nerves
Breathing

Get your breathing right first. When we are under stress, our breathing often becomes shallow. This is not enough breath for proper control, and this is why the simple act of breathing so often results in a gulp or a tremor.

> **A three-minute breathing exercise:**
>
> **Stand up and place your hands so that the fingertips are just touching each other over your diaphragm, which is located an inch or so above your waist. Keep your shoulders down and breathe in very slowly, being aware of drawing the breath from the diaphragm area. If you are doing it correctly, your fingertips will part from the fingertips of the other hand by about an inch. Now very slowly release the breath through your mouth, making a whooshing sound and making sure that it is a very long breath – significantly longer than the in-breath. Don't strain at it – it should feel natural. Repeat for about three minutes.**

If you still find that you feel nervous try this additional technique. On the in-breath, say to yourself, very slowly, "I – am – …" and on the outbreath, even more slowly, "relaxed…"

Visualizing

This is another useful technique, and one of the best methods I know of making sure that nervousness does not spoil your chances of getting the job. It's a technique now widely used by athletes and others before an important event.

Creating an image of success

Set aside at least 20 minutes somewhere totally quiet. Think back to an occasion where you felt confident, in charge, and at your best. Having identified the occasion, now call up an image of yourself as if you were watching yourself on a big cinema screen. See all the detail of what you were wearing, how you sat or stood and what was in the room. Hear again all the sounds in the room in every detail; call up the expressions on the other people's faces; remember exactly how you felt; what your bodily sensations were, and so on. This should take at least five minutes – take your time.

Once you have this image and all its associated sounds and feelings, make sure it's in full color in your mind. Now freeze the image so that it becomes a still frame. At the same time press your index finger and thumb together. This gives you a trigger association. Go through this process several times until it's routine. When you are approaching the interview, press your index finger and thumb together and recall the confident image and with it, the confident mental state you experienced on the original occasion.

The mental rehearsal

This is different from the practice interview. Again, set aside some quiet time – at least half an hour. What you are going to do is to play the whole interview in your head as if it were a private video-screening.

■ You are going to see yourself coming confidently into the room, smiling and greeting the panel.
■ Observe yourself sitting in an alert but relaxed way.
■ Hear yourself giving good answers to all the likely questions, in the actual time this will take.
■ Notice how the panel are responding positively to you. ·
■ See yourself leave, knowing you have given a good account of yourself.

The more detail you can fill in, the more effective this process is. It works because your mental association is with success rather than fear.

Mental rehearsal with a partner

Another way to use this technique is to ask a partner or friend to help you. In this variant, you are going to ask the friend to help you enter a light trance state where your unconscious mind is more open to suggestion.

■ Set aside some time when you can be sure of being uninterrupted. Ideally dim the lights.
■ Give the partner or friend the "script" on the left, and ask them to read it back to you slowly, in a quiet, even voice.
■ Allow time for the "questioning" part of the interview. Tell your partner that silence is fine at this stage of the process.
■ You close your eyes and concentrate on the words, conjuring up the images, sounds, and feelings that the words evoke.
■ At the end ask the partner to say, "now open your eyes" and slowly come back to reality.

Again, as with all these techniques, this works – your mind is focused on success, not failure.

3

A social event
Assessment centers
Presentations

The evidence-based technique

Things never to say or do

Asking your questions

Confirmation of date and time

When you are invited to attend the interview, make sure that you confirm in writing that you will be coming. Like many of the points in this book, this one seems obvious, but it is ignored by many candidates. It is not enough to call to confirm – ideally you should both call and write.

You may need to call in any case to negotiate the time slot for your appointment. The ideal time slots are just before lunch and towards the end of the process – not at the beginning nor at the very end. This is because interview panels are still getting into gear early on, and may be tired by the very end. Immediately after lunch is not a good idea either if you can avoid it as human beings seem to be designed to sleep then, and if the panel has treated itself to a large lunch to fortify itself, you may have even more of a struggle to convince them that you are their person.

If you can't make it

Some organizations are inflexible about both time and date. If there is a large panel, it may have taken weeks to find a date when everyone can be free. Unless they are very taken with your application, if you cannot make the appointed date, they may simply rule you out – or else politely tell you that if they do not choose one of the current candidates they may wish to return to you.

If you change your mind about being interviewed, tell the employer immediately. This is only courteous as they may want to rearrange times for other candidates, if there is time. Also, you may want to re-apply to the organization again at some point in the future.

Getting there

This is a simple point, but it's worth a reminder. If the interview is being held at a place you haven't previously visited, make sure you have:

- Directions on how to get there from someone who has been there already.
- A map, if needed.
- Knowledge of where to park, if you are driving.
- Allowed enough time to arrive unflustered, go to the bathroom, check your appearance and have a final glance at your notes. On balance, it is probably best to aim to arrive about half an hour before the interview. If you are early, the panel may also be running early – for instance, it is not uncommon for interviewees to withdraw at the last moment, leaving a hole in the schedule. In this case, if you arrive during the time the missing candidate should have been interviewed, you will probably have the advantage of being able to have a longer interview.

What to take in with you

You should plan to go into the interview with a folder of notes, including your application form (in a briefcase if you wish) and nothing else. It is usually perfectly safe to leave coat, handbag, gloves, scarves with whomever is looking after the outer-office or ante-room. This means you look calm and professional, and will also be undistracted by having to figure out where to put your coat, car keys, and so on.

> I once sat on a panel which was meeting a few days before Christmas. By far the strongest candidate nearly lost the job because she entered the interview room laden with shopping bags from a Toys R Us store, only a short distance away. In the post-interview discussion, the Panel Chair commented sourly that he supposed the only reason she'd agreed to be interviewed was in order to do her Christmas shopping.

The interview as a two-way process

When my colleagues and I coach people for job interviews, we notice how often people use remarkably extravagant language to describe their fears. These fears usually fall into a number of familiar categories:

- **Losing face.**
- **Drying up.**
- **Losing control.**
- **Being unable to stop talking once initial nerves have passed.**
- **Being inappropriately dressed.**
- **Failure: not getting a job they badly want.**
- **Getting the job and being afraid of doing it badly.**
- **Being offered a job it turns out they don't want after all.**

One source of all this fear can be that your mental model of the interview is that it is a one-way process: you may not feel that you have any power. In fact you have a lot of power in the interview.

If you are easily the best candidate, the employer may even feel that the power is all yours because if he or she likes you, then the reckoning will be that you may be equally attractive to another employer.

Remind yourself that you have already overcome several of the hurdles that the employer has put in place. Not every candidate is seen and it is unlikely that the employer will want to waste time seeing you if he or she does not think that you could do the job. In my work with employers, I always encourage them to see fewer rather than more candidates at interview, simply because of the high cost in time and money of the interview process.

And if you could do the job for this employer, then possibly you could do the job for another employer or even decide that you want to stay where you are. Being interviewed for another job is well known as a sort of polite blackmailing tactic to force an existing employer to raise a salary or find a more attractive job. When you go into the interview, remember that the employer does not know whether this could be true for you.

Balance of power

When you sit on the other side of the interview process, this power balance is even easier to see. I was once part of a panel interviewing for a senior post in a medium-sized organization.

Although there was an apparently strong shortlist of people, all of whom were appointable in theory, it immediately became clear that there was one outstanding candidate. He had been laid off from his previous job, so there was a natural tendency on the part of the panel to assume that there would be a degree of panic on his part. He was impeccably pleasant and courteous throughout the whole interview.

In its closing stages, there was the usual conversation about when and how candidates would be informed of the panel's decision. The Panel Chair said that there could be a short delay as one candidate still had to be seen on a different day. At this stage the candidate very politely said: "I appreciate your difficulty, but I've already been offered another quite attractive job, so I'd really welcome an early decision."

The interview is not a trial

After the candidate had left the room, it was the panel who fell into panic mode. "We've got to have him. How can we stop him accepting the other job?" In no time at all it had been agreed that the remaining candidate's interview would be pushed up on the schedule, and by the end of the following day the original strong candidate had been offered the job, his desirability immeasurably increased because it was clear he was attractive to another employer. Here, the onus was very much on the potential employer to seem attractive to the candidate, not the other way around.

The interview is not a courtroom where you are on trial. Nor have you been captured and taken into enemy territory, where you are going to be subjected to a brutal and humiliating interrogation. On the contrary, the job interview is an exploratory conversation where you and a potential employer size each other up.

The interview as a two-way process

Your task during the time you are with them is to ask yourself:

■ What can I tell about the organization /department/unit by the way they are treating me? Have I been treated courteously or discourteously? Formally or informally? Efficiently or sloppily? For instance, you might want to think twice about joining a company that kept you waiting for your interview in a cold room without refreshment or any apparent concern for your welfare.

■ What do I think about the person who would be my supervisor if I get this job? Could I work with him or her? Would he or she have my respect? The potential supervisor is easily the most important person at the interview: pay special attention here.

■ What can I tell about this organization/department/unit from the way people behave? How do they dress? What kind of atmosphere is there? Would I fit in and be happy here? A thorough and professional selection process will give you the chance to meet potential team-mates. Are these people you would enjoy working with as colleagues?

Where you have any doubts about the answers, listen to them. Never accept a job offer just because you feel flattered and relieved that someone wants you. Ask for an informal further meeting. The more senior the job, the more common this is.

It's not by chance that the pompous-sounding 'executive search' process for senior vacancies is more usually described as "head-hunting." The implication is that you are the head – the prized scalp that is to be brought home through cunning: lured, persuaded, cajoled. Unpleasant though the basic metaphor is, it is actually a more truthful representation of what really goes on in any job interview, however humble the job. It is actually a courtship. You have to be courted by the organization, just as much as they have to be courted by you.

The interview as a social event

There is some evidence to suggest that the interview, as traditionally conducted, can really only give a panel two kinds of information about the candidates they see:

- Their social skills
- Their motivation: do they really want the job?

Some points to remember: My experience certainly reinforces the likely truth of this. Time and again I have seen the job go to the candidate with good social skills and enthusiasm. These candidates instinctively realize that the interview is a social occasion. The panel are the hosts and you are the guest. Their role is to make you feel comfortable so that you can sell yourself to them. Your role is to make them feel comfortable so that they can sell themselves to you.

Your behavior affects other people's response to you. Smile and the interview panel will smile back.

How do you display good social skills in the interview? Here are some of the things it's most important to do:

- Smile. If you look tense and serious you will make the panel feel tense. There has been research showing that the person who smiles the most is the one most likely to get the job.

- Involve the entire panel in your questions and answers by constantly engaging them with eye contact.

- Convey relaxed confidence and alertness in how you sit.

- Sit upright – not rigid – but with your bottom tucked into the back of the chair, hands folded neatly into your lap and feet firmly planted on the floor. Keep your shoulders down.

- Don't slump, cross your legs or arms; don't sit on the edge of your chair or sideways in it.

Personal experience as an interviewer of how candidates should not do it includes examples of both over and under-confidence:

• A candidate who spent the whole interview slouching with one arm casually flung across the back of his chair so that he was only half-facing the panel.

• A candidate who was so nervous that she looked anywhere but at the panel for most of the 40 minutes she was in the room.

The interview as a social event

Share the talking. The ideal is 50:50. You are gathering information about them, as much as they are gathering it about you.

Keep your answers brief. A good guest does not bore the host by going on at length with some anecdote, and neither should you. The absolute maximum length of any reply should be three minutes. One and a half to two minutes is better. If you're unsure how long two minutes sounds, then make that part of your practice interview. In fact, as advertisers know, it's possible to say an awful lot in just 30 seconds! If you give long replies, the panel tends to think: "This person is too fond of the sound of their own voice." If your replies are ultra-brief, the panel may think you lack confidence. If in doubt about the length of your answer, it is perfectly OK to pause and say: "Is this about the right amount of detail?" Take your cue from the panel's response. If you are going on too long, they will be pleased at the chance to stop your discourse. If you're being too brief with your answers, they will encourage you to say more.

Speak clearly and without jargon. This is especially important where the panel contains members who are not specialists in your area. It irritates the non-specialist to hear jargon – it makes them feel excluded and marginalized and they may attribute motives to you such as wanting to show off or being vain or arrogant.

The importance of rapport

Because the interview is a social event, your task is to create a rapport with the interviewer, just as it is his or her task to create a rapport with you. When conversation is flowing you are much more likely to be the person who gets the job.

How do you know rapport when you see it? Look at two people who are getting on well together and you will see that they are mirroring each other. They will sit at exactly similar angles to each other, use similar gestures, cross their legs or scratch their noses at the same time. If they are in a bar, they will lift their glasses at the same moment and the drink will go down in the glasses at the same rate. Ideally you need to do the equivalent at the interview.

Matching

Rapport is about matching. Mostly we do this unconsciously, but skilled behavior at interviews is about raising the most effective behavior from the subconscious and keeping it under control in spite of nerves and tension. If you mismatch, you will be creating discomfort for the interviewer and will decrease your chances of getting the job.

Rapport means that you are demonstrating respect for the other person. How do you create this? It's really not what you actually say, though that is important too. It all really depends on what you do with your non-verbal signals.

Keep your voice up – many candidates allow nervousness to reduce their volume to little more than a whisper. Some go to the opposite extreme and bellow. If you know you are prone to either of these traps, practice the correct volume beforehand. It may be one of the most important areas to get feedback on from whoever is your practice interviewer.

Other tips for creating rapport

Look at the way the interviewer is sitting and try to make sure that you match his or her body language. So, for instance, if he or she is sitting forward, you should lean slightly forward too, as you answer the questions.

Interviewers vary in the way they speak. If your interviewer speaks quickly and enthusiastically, you should try to do the same. If he or she speaks more slowly and deliberately, you should try matching that.

Gesture: some interviewers wave their arms around dramatically, some are more contained. Matching is not about copying – that could seem insulting – but some discreet matching can be helpful. If you know, for instance, that you tend to sit very still, then you could run the risk of mismatching an interviewer who has extravagant gestures.

Interview questions

There are whole books on answering interview questions, but experience shows that there are really only eight questions that can be asked at interviews. They may be expressed in hundreds of different ways, but this is what they come down to:

1 What are you currently doing? (Your present job or how you are spending your time if unemployed).

2 **Why do you want this job?**

3 Why do you want to work in this organization/department/unit?

4 **What skills and experience do you have that fit our needs? How will your skills help you to do this job to a high standard?**

5 How would you tackle this job? What are your ideas about changing or improving the way this role is carried out?

6 **What kind of person are you? What stresses you? What delights you?**

7 Do your personal circumstances fit with what we need? (e.g. frequent travel).

8 **What questions would you like to ask us?**

Prepare your answers

You need to have built comprehensive answers into your preparation. Give the list to the friend who is running your practice interview and encourage him or her to create two or three questions around each area.

Below, there are three keys to answering these questions successfully:

- Your research into the job and organization (see p.18).
- Demonstrating a giving not a taking attitude.
- Using evidence from your experience to answer questions.

Giving, not taking

Employers hate feeling exploited. They dread taking on staff who turn out to be constantly taking sick days, who are determined to leave on the dot of 5 p.m. or who insist on taking their vacations every year in certain weeks and whose concern is for themselves, not their colleagues or the company as a whole.

As an interviewee, you must convey that you are a giver not a taker. You need to show:

- Enthusiasm for the mission of organization/department/unit
- Commitment and enthusiasm for the work
- Flexibility
- Sympathy for the challenges of organization/departments/units
- Ability to solve problems, not create them
- Resourcefulness

Some examples

Questions	Takers	Givers
"Why do you want this job?"	SAY: *"Because it will be good for my career."*	SAY: *"Because I think I have x and y to offer here"* – and describe it.
"What's the most important thing about any job for you?"	SAY: *"A good salary,"* or *"security."*	SAY: *"The chance to work on really interesting problems, or, to do something of practical benefit to people."*
"What do you want to ask us?"	SAY: *"How much vacation would I get?"* or, *"What percentage contribution do you make to the employees' 401k plan?"*	SAY: *"I'm interested in what you see as the trends on x or y issue."*
"What are the main problems facing this organization/unit?"	SAY: *"They are so serious that it's hard to see how to get around them."*	SAY: *"There are exciting and challenging times ahead. My ideas would be…"*

Using the evidence-based technique

The panel can't know how you would actually do the job – they are speculating, and so are you. Easily the most effective way to convince them that you would do the job well is to offer evidence of past behavior.

Wise, not smart, answers:

This is how it works. Suppose you are asked: "What's the thing you are most proud of in your current job?" You may be tempted to reply with something like "having a job at all." This would be a smart, but not a wise answer.

All your replies must quote evidence from your experience which links with the skill the employer is looking for. Let's suppose in this case that the job specifies skill in negotiating – you know this because you have been sent the "person specification" (see p. 21).

Your ideal reply

"*I'm most proud of managing a really tricky negotiation with our union. I led our team and…*" You then go on to describe what happened.

Another example

The interviewer asks, "*How do you know you could manage this unit effectively while still meeting all of its budgetary targets?*" The unwise reply would be, "*My attitude is that it is critically important and I would set the right kinds of controls in place.*"

This tells the interviewer something about the attitude you claim, but nothing about what you actually do. So the wise reply would be to link it with your specific past experience of budgetary management, the closer the better to what you understand this job to need.

How to use the evidence-based technique

- Be specific not general.
- Describe what you personally did and the impact this action had. So for instance, if asked: "*What did you contribute to the set-up phase of Project X?*", you would say: "*I set up the whole project from start to finish – it was my idea, so I obtained the necessary resources and did all the initial planning with a project team I had chosen myself. We looked at everything and anything that could go wrong and assessed all the risks, financial and otherwise. The result was that the project got off to a very smooth start because we had done all the hard thinking at the outset.*"
- Don't be afraid to bring in volunteer activities if your professional experience is lacking in some particular area.
- Remember, you're describing what happened – not your personal attitudes or ideas.

A final example

"What's your attitude to being in a team?"

Unwise reply:

"I love it – I'm sure I'd settle in here."

Wise reply:

"My present job requires really close team work because we each depend on everyone else to get particular work done (then you describe how you currently contribute and what effect that has on the whole team), so I'm very positive about team work."

Funnelling down

Note that properly trained interviewers are shown how to get evidence from candidates. They use a technique sometimes called "funnelling down." This goes in the following way. A candidate is asked a question such as: *"Tell us about your approach to managing a major change in your team – give us an example from something you've recently dealt with."*

Let's suppose that an untrained candidate gives a rather vague reply such as: *"We've had a lot of change recently and it's been very hard to get all the staff on board, but I think we did it OK because people seem to have settled down a bit now."*

The trained interviewer is not going to be satisfied with a reply like this because it does not give any evidence of what the candidate's own responsibility or achievements were. So there will be a follow-up question which obliges the candidate to narrow down the answer. This might go something like: *"Yes, I see, but what did you specifically do to help that happen?"*

It is hard to wriggle out of an evidence-based reply when pressed like this.

When you are lucky enough to meet a properly trained interviewer, then you will find that you are politely probed for evidence in this way. If you are also trained along the lines described here, then the process will happen smoothly for both sides.

Most interviewers are not trained, and so you will probably have to manage this for them.

Things never to say or do at an interview

A good many candidates destroy their chances of getting the job through sheer clumsiness:

- The senior manager who did not get the chief executive job he craved. One reason was that he was disrespectful of his current boss at the interview.

- The young secretary so desperate to get into publishing that she turned her job title into "Editorial Assistant" and lied at the interview about her experience. She was exposed when the employer sent a routine request for confirmation to her current employer.

- The training consultant who prattled on artlessly and inaccurately about a major change program, involving training at the airline at which she worked, without ever realizing that she was talking to one of the main architects of the change (who by then had changed jobs and organizations).

- Lying: there is a strong chance you will be found out, especially if the job is in a related field where people do a lot of networking. Sometimes the deceit is discovered in unusual ways. In one recent example, an employee took her employers to the local labor board, claiming unfair dismissal. The board agreed, but reduced the damages considerably on the grounds that she had lied about her qualifications – a Bachelor's degree from a major university turned out to be a certificate of completion from a correspondence school. It is always best to tell the truth and to resist the temptation to inflate your qualifications or experience. If found out, you could lose the job. Employers are quite rightly sticklers for honesty.

- Asking for 25 percent or 50 percent more than the advertised salary. Never negotiate salary at the interview (see p. 65). Asking for a much bigger salary irritates employers and may suggest you are too full of yourself or that if offered the job, you will leave as soon as you get a better offer. Don't apply for the job if you really couldn't work around the salary mentioned, plus or minus 10 percent.

So here is a brief checklist of thing to AVOID at all costs:

- "My current boss is an idiot."

- "My present boss and I have a personality clash."
  Employer reaction: If you're that disloyal to your current boss, the chances are that you'll be the same in any other job.

- "I can't wait to leave my present job."
  Employer reaction: as above.

- "My present colleagues get on my nerves."
  Employer reaction: this is someone who can't work in a team.

- "My current salary is…" (naming an inflated amount.) This is one thing employers always check with referees.

- Inflating your experience. If you inflate your experience, a skilled interviewer will ruthlessly expose how little you know through using the interview and question techniques described in this book.

An employer who has any doubt about the truth of what you claim is likely to check this through a telephone conversation with your current employer.

- Improving the sound of your job title. Even the laziest employer will check this with your current employer.

- Lying about qualifications. Several recent high-profile cases have highlighted the need for employers to check qualifications. It is very simple for the employer to do – one telephone call is all it needs. Most employers are less interested in qualifications than you may think. Experience is usually considered a lot more important, so resist the temptation to improve the look of your CV.

- Fictionalizing your interests. The point of putting interests on your CV is to represent yourself as an all-around person, not just a work person. Don't put down opera if your real interest is sitting on the couch at home watching TV. It will only take one question to expose you.

Things never to say or do at an interview

Wiser tactics

- Always be respectful and positive about your current boss, even if the relationship has been stormy. The potential new boss may know the present boss. It's a smaller world than you may think.
- Speak enthusiastically about your present subordinates. If you criticize them, it will reflect badly on you because it was your responsibility to coach and develop them. Avoid criticizing current colleagues and bosses under any circumstances – for any reason.
- Similarly, talk enthusiastically about current team-mates. After all, you have been part of that team and will have made a contribution to whatever the current team climate is. All potential bosses know this.
- Make sure that you can back up anything you claim about your opinions at the interview. For instance, if asked a question about what you are reading, never claim you are reading a book which you only know about through reading the reviews. You may be asked a follow-up question which reveals that your knowledge is skin deep or even less.

- Don't claim experience which you don't actually have. A skilled interviewer will probe until he or she is satisfied about your involvement and knowledge. If this is so small as to be minuscule, you will be shown up.
- Give accurate job titles. Don't be tempted to turn a "manager" job into a "head of" job.
- If asked for your education details, put them down correctly. Don't turn Harvard Technical Institute into Harvard University.
- Make sure that you have listed your qualifications accurately, including awarding bodies and dates. Employers are now checking them as a matter of routine.

Coping with incompetent interviewers

ncompetent interviewers don't do it on purpose. They may be inexperienced, nervous, or over-confident. They may blunder innocently into areas in which the law forbids questions. Below and on the following pages are some of the main ways in which interviewer incompetence shows through, together with some suggested ways of dealing with it:

1. Double or even triple questions

This is probably the most common single mistake. Here's an example:
'I wonder if you can tell me what experience you have of leading a team and also whether you've actually ever had any training in team leadership?'
This is two questions rolled into one.

How to deal with it

Politely re-phrase the questions – not to humiliate the interviewer – but to remind yourself of the questions. Say something like: *"I'll deal with the two aspects separately if I may – my team leadership experience first, then my training."*

You may find, as many people do, that you forget one of the questions. If this happens, say: *"I'm afraid I've forgotten the first (or second) half of the question. Can you just remind me of it please?"*

2. The rambling question

The interviewer who rambles at length has forgotten, or never knew, that the purpose of the interview is to listen, to hear you talk and to respond to the questions you will have.

How to deal with it

Listen really carefully. The actual question will be buried somewhere inside the rambling.

Summarize what you think the question is by saying something like: *"Can I just check that I'm understanding your question properly? You believe that many people in senior jobs don't know how to read a balance sheet, and you'd like me to show you that I do?"*

Coping with incompetent interviewers

3. The hypothetical question

Trained interviewers know that they have to avoid hypothetical questions. Untrained interviewers love them.

Hypothetical questions are a bad idea for a number of reasons. The first is that they give unfair advantage to internal candidates. For instance, a candidate looking for a job as a residential care worker was asked: *"What would you do if a resident locked himself in his room and threatened to set fire to it?"* She used the evidence-based technique (see p. 44–45) to answer, describing how she handled real crises. She got the job. However, later she was teased for not knowing the "right" answer, which was that the staff kept duplicate keys. There was, of course, no way she could have known this.

The second reason is that they only test your ability to give a smart answer, not what you would actually do if the hypothetical situation became real. Finally, it is most unlikely that the exact hypothetical situation would happen, therefore it is neither here nor there what you reply.

How to deal with it

DON'T
- Criticize the interviewer openly for asking a clumsy question.
- Fall into the trap of trying to give a hypothetical answer.

DO
- Say something like: *"It's difficult to say how I would deal with that because I'm sure once I was in the job, it would be affected by what I then knew about your systems and so on. But I can talk about an occasion in my current job when I dealt with something very similar."*

You then describe the past situation, fitting it as closely to whatever the interviewer's concern seems to be.
- If you don't have any matching experience that you can quote, use the first part of the answer (left) then: *"...knew about your systems and so on. But in general, my attitude to this kind of situation is to..."*

Hypothetical questions are usually about crises. You could reply that you would look for underlying causes, not knee-jerk responses.

4. The politically incorrect question

This interviewer has never heard of any of the legislation concerning equal opportunities. He or she, more usually he, feels it is perfectly all right to press women candidates for answers to questions such as:

- *What are your plans about having children?*
- *What are your childcare arrangements?*
- *Are you actually divorced?*
- *What happens if your children are ill?*

How to deal with it

DON'T

- Threaten to report him to the Equal Employment Opportunities Commission (EEOC).
- Get on your moral high horse, however tempting it may be.
- Tell him he needs training or consciousness-raising.
- Ask if he is asking the male (or white) candidates the same question(s).
- Storm out of the interview indignantly.

DO

Stay calm and friendly, but note that the question may reveal an environment which is male-dominated, naively sexist or racist or one where it is difficult for women to progress. On the other hand it may reveal no such things, but it will be worth investigating before you accept any job offer.

Deal with the underlying concern, which is: *"What are your priorities?" "Will you be off work a lot?" "Can you really do the job?"* Possible answers could include: *"My family is very important to me, but so is my work. I've always made sure that I've had excellent childcare arrangements,"* or, *"I take my responsibility to my employer very seriously. I haven't had any days off other than scheduled vacations for two years,"* or, *"Well, I wouldn't want to bore you with my domestic arrangements, but they satisfy me and if they can do that, I think they'll be OK for you!"*

Other politically incorrect interviewers may question:

- Single people about their sexual orientation.
- Older people about their health.
- Disabled people about their mobility.

Coping with incompetent interviewers

5. The "model" answer

Government agencies and authorities – local, state, and federal – are the main offenders here. In the late 70s and early 80s, local authorities became obsessed by political correctness. A lot of anxiety focused, probably rightly, on the selection interview. Unfortunately, although the diagnosis was correct (i.e. interviewing had previously been the source of biased and unfair selection decisions) the solution adopted has not helped. In the model-answer approach, a set of rigid questions is agreed and a model answer is actually written down for the panel. Often, follow-up probe questions – one of the expert interviewer's most useful tools – are expressly forbidden. Even more ridiculously, I know of at least one local authority where interviewers are trained to show no emotion whatever towards candidates, including smiling and nodding. Absurdly, this is supposed to make it easier to compare one candidate with another.

Model answers are a bad idea for similar reasons to the hypothetical question. They favor the internal candidate because the internal candidate is more likely to have warning of what kinds of things it is OK or not OK to say. Model answers also encourage people to answer in the way they think the interviewer wants to hear. In other words, your effort goes into trying to second guess the panel rather than in demonstrating that you could do the job.

How to deal with it

You can't deal with it directly, as you may not know until later that the panel was using this approach, although you may guess that this is the case from the stilted way the questions are asked. Another give-away is the lack of follow-up questions. Two tactics do help: Use the evidence-based technique (p. 44–45) where the quality of what you offer will usually suffice. In effect, you oblige the panel to appoint you, in spite of their self-imposed limitations.

Have your USP prepared (p. 24–25) and use it at some appropriate moment in the interview. Make maximum use of the part of the interview which deals with *"What questions do you have for us?"* by saying: *"I'd like to take a moment just to draw attention to one or two aspects of my experience that I think it would be useful for you to hear about"* – and then briefly describe them.

{
6. The off-the-wall questions
The questioner who talks all the time
The questioner who wants a nice chat

I have bracketed these three together because they are variants of the same thing: nervous interviewers who try to escape from their apprehension.

They do this by avoiding giving you the chance to talk about the things that really count – your experience, your skills your personality and any new ideas you can bring to the organization. They want you to do well, but they are afraid you might not. In response:

How to deal with it

DON'T

Don't collude. Doing this means taking the unwise option of going along with the interviewer and turning the whole thing into a low-key chat.

For instance, a former colleague of mine went for an interview as a controller to someone she knew socially for a "chat about the job".

She emerged from this occasion totally bemused. Nothing had been said about the nature of the business other than what she already knew, or what her duties would be. She took the job, but it turned out to be a mistake. She wanted a job with greater responsibility and he really only wanted a glorified bookkeeper.

In other words, colluding will deprive you of the chance to find out what the job is actually about, and what skills you will need for it.

DO

Politely take a degree of control by briefly acknowledging whatever the interviewer has said, but then turning your answer to how your experience fits the job in relation to whatever issue the interviewer has raised.

Use the *"have you any questions"* part of the interview to say something like: *"I feel I haven't really said much about some aspects of why I'd like this job and why my experience is suitable for it – could I take a few moments to do that?"* If you get a nod of assent here, then plunge into a suitably shortened version of what you would have said if you'd been asked more focussed questions. If you can carry it off, look for the tiny pauses in the interviewer's flow where you can break in. This, however, is a high-risk strategy as it may look rude if it is seen as "interrupting."

Nervous interviewers are more afraid of the interview process than they are of not appointing the right person. They rarely realize how off-putting their questioning approach can be. These are the interviewers whose own dread is of drying up or of not being able to think of clever questions. When a nervous interviewer meets a nervous interviewee, the result can be dire. It is almost certain that a good appointment will not be made.

Coping with incompetent interviewers

7. The leading question

The leading question is the one that suggests a right answer, often "yes" or "no". An example would be: *"I'm sure you'd never make the mistake of failing to do appraisals for your staff?"*

It is generally asked by the panel member who is impressed by you and wants to convince other panel members that you are the best candidate.

The leading question is a poor way to ask candidates about their experience because it does not probe, nor does it look for the experience which shows whether the candidate can actually do what the job needs. Panel members who are still making up their minds will not find a "yes" or "no" or other brief answer to a leading question very convincing.

How to deal with it

DON'T

Just reply with a single word or phrase. If you do this you will again lose an opportunity to put your views. Other members of the panel may also think you lack courage – they may not necessarily agree with the opinions their colleague is expressing and will want to hear your own views.

DO

Look for the underlying pre-occupation. An example was the interviewer who asked a candidate: *"Wouldn't you agree that leadership and management are two different things and that most organizations are over-managed and underled?"*

The unwise answer would have been: *"Oh yes, I completely agree. Most organizations really do lack leadership."* She interpreted the question, rightly, as being about whether or not she was familiar with the distinction between leadership and management, so she replied: *"Yes I agree, but perhaps that's because managing people through change is much more challenging than just keeping the systems and processes going. I try to be able to do both, but it's change I'm really interested in. Would it be useful if I said more about my approach here?"*

A second tactic is to turn the question into an open one. So if the interviewer says, *"I suppose that leading a team is pretty challenging?"*, you could reply: *"Yes, it is. My own approach to it has been..."* And then you describe your own experiences.

Awkward questions: some answers

Answering awkward questions

Like virtually all candidates, you may have something in your job history that you believe could disadvantage you. If it is obvious from your CV, as 99 percent of the time it is, the general rules are simple:

- Don't deny it or lie; you will be found out.
- Stay calm – the employer may care a lot less about it than you think.
- Focus your answer firmly on the future – whatever the disadvantage is, it is now in the past and you are fully able to do the job.

Here are some examples. It's not an exhaustive list, but it will give you the idea.

A poor health record/disability

Employer fear: you'll be out sick a lot.

You're fully recovered and totally energetic or your condition is under control with medication/special treatment and need not prevent you working as a full member of the team.

A large number of jobs in a short period

Employer fear: you won't stay.

You have deliberately had a number of short-term jobs as a way of finding out what it is you really want to do – and now you know that, you want to stay put and give your all.

A very long time in one organization/job

Employer fear: you're inflexible, fixed on how they did things in your old organization.

The work in your old organization was interesting enough to keep you there. Although it may look like one job, in fact you held a wide variety of responsibilities… But now it's time to move on and you are looking forward to a change.

Awkward questions: some answers

A period of having been laid off/ unemployed

Employer fear: you're unemployable; there's something risky about you; you've forgotten how to do a job.

With so many large companies downsizing, it's inevitable that even good people lose their jobs. You've used the time fruitfully to study, plant a garden…etc. Now you're raring to go again, feel you have a lot to offer…

A former boss with whom he/she suspects you did not get on

Employer fear: this is someone who finds it difficult to accept authority.

Say nothing to the discredit of the former boss. Describe their good points and emphasize how much you learned from working with them.

A prison sentence

Employer fear: you might get into trouble again.

If you've got as far as the interview, this is an enlightened person. Say you've paid your debt to society, have acquired many new skills/attitudes – that's all in the past; your record since leaving prison shows how different you now are.

Your age

Employer fear: you're too old/ too young.

Though it may seem unusual for someone your age to be applying for the job, you are convinced you have the qualities needed (then describe them using evidence – see p. 44–45).

Your biggest mistake

Employer fear: you are too arrogant to continue learning.

Briefly describe a relatively insignificant mistake (not the sort that can bring a whole organization to its knees) and put the emphasis on what you learned from it, and why you will never do that one again.

Your major weakness

Employer hope: you will shoot yourself in the foot.

Choose something that could also be a strength – for instance preferring working with the big picture rather than the detail, or cramming too much into your day.

Another useful tactic is to refer to something which was a weakness in the past, but which you have now conquered. For instance, you might say something like: *"I know that when I first started being a (name the job title) I found it difficult to prioritize because I'm energetic and wanted to get so much done. But that was ten years ago and I think I've more than got that aspect of my work under control now to do the job I now do!"*

This question is often asked in the plural: *"Tell us about your weaknesses."* Beware of falling into the trap of providing several examples. One is quite enough!

Your views on a controversial current affairs issue

Employer fear: you are in a little world of your own and have no knowledge of current affairs. Or if you do, you are a prejudiced person.

The safe answer is to convey that you can see both sides of a very complicated question. There is no easy solution and a thoughtful person would take time to consider long-term implications of any ideas on the topic.

General tips on answering awkward questions

The awkward question puts you on the spot and the danger is that you could feel your confidence crumbling. Many people find it difficult to be assertive and speak up for themselves. The approved social behavior is to be modest, perhaps excessively so, and not claim too much or "blow your own horn." To appear boastful is definitely counter to this lifelong training. However, the interview is not the place for modesty. The keys to success are:

■ Use direct language
Watch out for the use of would-be modest phrases like:
"I'm pretty sure I could lead this team effectively."
"I think I'm quite good at…"
This sort of tentative language is all right when you are discussing yourself with your boss or with friends, but it is no good at an interview. Qualifying phrases make you sound as if you doubt your own abilities.
Instead, use direct language:
"I can lead a successful team."
"I am good at leading a team."
"I know I do x or y well."

■ Give yourself references from others
Where you find it hard to be direct, consider using phrases which in effect quote what other people have said about you. For instance, if you are asked about your style as a manager, say something like:
"My team tells me that since I arrived on the scene I have transformed the whole atmosphere in the office by …"
"I get a lot of feedback about my style from my colleagues at work. They say that …"
"At my last performance review my boss told me that he really likes the way I have tried to create a democratic atmosphere within my own team."

Asking your own questions

By tradition, the final part of the interview is the one where the panel chair asks you what questions you would like to ask. As with every other aspect of the interview, you need to play this with sensitivity. If the panel members are shuffling uneasily and looking at their watches, you know they are running late, or possibly have lost interest in you, so keep your questions brief. If they are looking relaxed and attentive, you could safely assume there is more time.

There are two good reasons for taking advantage of the chance to ask questions:

■ It's the part of the interview where you are unequivocally in control.
■ It's another chance to demonstrate your unique qualities, experience, and resourcefulness.

Always have some questions prepared. It's perfectly all right to take out your notes at this point. Look for ways to link things that have been said by panel members to the questions you want to ask. For instance: *"I noticed earlier on you mentioned the appraisal system, I'd like to ask you some more about that."*

Another example might be: *"When I replied to your question about training, you commented that... could you tell me a little more about that?"*

This shows how carefully you have been listening during the interview, and not just looking on it as a chance for you to talk.

The questions themselves should be about the organization and the job and should be based on your pre-interview research. Ideally they will be present or future-based questions such as:

■ How will you judge how the person you appoint is successful in the job?
■ What's the likely policy on x or y in the future?
■ What percentage of market share do you aim for in x or y brands?
■ What kind of morale is there in the department at the moment?

Things to avoid:

- Don't ask questions about: salary, pension plan, contract-length, vacation and holiday schedule, health insurance program, company cars. The appropriate time to do this is when you have actually been offered the job (see p. 85).
- Don't ask questions that have already been answered earlier in the interview.
- Don't say: *"I don't have any questions,"* as this can be taken as passivity or lack of interest.
- Perhaps the most important don't of all is this: don't start interviewing the interviewer. This has several effects: it breaks the convention that you are the interviewee and they are the interviewers; it looks rude; it may come across as hostile; it may suggest you think you have the job in the bag.

As a boss I once interviewed a promising candidate for a job. Although I noted a slight tendency to talk too much during the interview, I still thought she was a strong candidate. We got to the final part of the ritual and I asked: *"What questions do you have for us?"* She took out a stout file and embarked on an attempt to grill and cross-question us about the culture of the department, whether or not people were happy and what we planned to do about it if they were not. As a final question she asked us for feedback on her performance as an interviewee. Fortunately, we were able to say politely but firmly that we had to curtail that part of the interview because we were falling behind in our schedule. We did not appoint her.

You may also like to use this part of the interview to add anything that you wanted to say but were not asked about by the employer. For instance, you might say: *"I don't have any other questions, but I think I may have under-emphasized my experience of x while you were asking me questions about that earlier. I'd just like to add that..."* (and then you describe your experience.)

One important question to ask is: *"When will you let me know what your decision is?"* This is vital information, as if you don't hear within the named time period, you should call to find out what is happening.

On-the-spot hire

As a young teacher looking for my first job, I remember vividly the torture of my first experience of being interviewed. I was called to a prep school in a small town in New England and told that my interview would be at 11a.m., but that there would be a tour of the school at 9a.m. with all the other candidates. It was explained that the decision would be made on the day, so I was expected to wait at the school until 4p.m., when the successful candidate would be offered the job.

I had never been to that part of the country before, and when I stepped off the train that morning I felt very isolated. I met the other candidates, all of whom seemed equally tongue-tied, was shown around the school without meeting any of the people with whom I would be working if I got the job.

The interview seemed to go quite well, but then there was a long, tedious wait while all the other candidates were interviewed. Conversation was desultory while we waited for the verdict.

Unfriendly practices

Teachers, hospital, and local government staff sometimes used to be selected in this crude and insensitive manner: all candidates were called for interview at the same time. All sat around for the entire day, going in one at a time for the interview. All sat nervously awaiting the decision. The door would open: Mr X, will you come in, please? Mr X would be offered the job and was expected to say "yes" on the spot and to agree a salary.

If he said "no," or "don't know," the number two choice would be called in. The reasons are that:

- Local politicians are usually involved and the assumption is that they need to see the whole process through from beginning to end.
- The panel presumes that candidates will be desperate for the job and will therefore submit to this process without complaint.

Unfortunately, there are still pockets of this candidate-unfriendly practice even today.

You may be unlucky enough to encounter it. If so, here is what to do:

■ Check in advance that this really is how the organization makes its selections. Call the human resources specialist, if there is one, and check what actually happens.

■ Decide whether you want to go ahead with the choice of being a candidate. Selecting people in such a way may suggest that this is an organization which is out of touch with current thinking. If you go ahead, do it knowingly.

■ Make doubly sure you research the job in advance. This means thoroughly checking out the previous job-holder, why he or she left, and what the job consists of.

■ Research the locality if it is different from the one where you are currently based. What does housing cost? What are the schools like? Is there adequate transportation?

■ Discuss it with your partner and family. Are they committed to your change of job if it will mean relocating residence, changing schools, etc?

■ Research the potential boss. What do people say about working with this person? Explore any tell-tale hints that he or she might be a bully or in a weak position.

■ Research the organization along the lines described on p. 18.

■ Make a list of the questions that you must ask at the interview. Take this list into the interview with you and make sure you ask them and push for satisfactory answers.

■ Be very clear what salary you want. You may also be asked to negotiate salary during the interview.

■ Use the waiting time to decide if you will say "yes" if the panel offer you the job.

■ If you are the strongest candidate, you could try negotiating for more time to think; don't be surprised, though, if they say "no."

■ Finally, you could consider saying "yes" at the time, while resolving to actually make up your mind later. This may make you uneasy, but it is, however, a pragmatic route that many candidates have taken.

Assessment centers

A minority of organizations approaches recruitment and selection with solemn and thorough professionalism. While this does not guarantee that they will be enjoyable places to work, it is a good sign. These organizations may devote one, two or more days to the selection process. They will invite you to something known as an Assessment Center. This may happen on the organization's premises or in a hotel.

The main thing to note is that everything you do is being observed. The techniques used will include:

- Timed ability tests – for instance of verbal reasoning and math proficiency. Take these steadily and quietly and read the instructions very carefully. It is possible to buy sample sets of similar tests at large bookstores and to practice at home before doing the Assessment Center. Research shows that it is possible to make significant improvements in your score through coaching for many of these tests. If you suspect that this may be a weakness, it will be worth the small investment involved and will also build your confidence.

- Timed aptitude tests – for instance whether you are capable of making fine visual discriminations; whether you can write a decent précis of a long document.

- Psychometric tests (or personality tests) which aim to give a snapshot picture of the kind of person you are. There is no point in trying to "cheat" by answering in the way you would like to be. Be honest. All reputable tests have honesty detectors built into them. Also, the better the test, the harder it is to guess what factors of personality it is actually measuring. It is usually best to answer questions quickly without pausing too much over them.

- In-tray exercises – usually confined to selection for managerial posts. Here you are given a set of documents which look like the contents of a busy manager's in-tray and asked to say how you would prioritize or deal with the various memos and letters.

What to look out for

As a candidate you should expect the following as good ethical practice in an assessment center where tests are used:

■ A test administrator who clearly explains the purpose of every test. It should never be a mystery.

■ Time allotted to reading and understanding the instructions – for instance, if a test is timed, whether there will be reminders of how the time is passing.

■ Clarity about what will happen to your test results – for instance who will see them and how long they will be stored.

■ Where the tests fit into the selection process. Beware of employers who make yes or no decisions on the basis of tests alone. You should expect to have any issues raised by the tests discussed with you at the final interview you attend.

■ Psychometric tests usually have no time limit.

■ The tests should be administered and interpreted by licensed practitioners. All leading test publishers make it difficult and costly for people to buy their tests and insist on rigorous training. This is to deter people from thinking of them as being just like a quiz in a magazine, and because the tests themselves have been developed out of many years of research. Furthermore, the most useful tests so far devised are subtle and need both intelligence and insight to interpret properly.

■ It is poor ethical practice to use tests used for one purpose as part of a selection process on a different occasion.

■ Provision for feedback. Giving individual feedback to candidates costs time and therefore money, especially if external consultants are being used. However, you should always be offered the chance to see reports and to discuss them with whoever is briefing the panel.

Assessment centers

The most common psychometric tests

■ The OPQ stands for Occupational Personality Questionnaire. It is widely used in the United Kingdom.
■ The 16PF stands for Sixteen Personality Factors
■ The CPI stands for California Personality Inventory.

There is also a test which is sometimes used called the Strong Interest Inventory, which links vocational interests to personality.

The aim of the tests

All ask you to fill in a questionnaire where you are asked to choose between two or more equally attractive types of answer. Essentially they are giving you many chances to answer the same question.

The best tests are more subtle than most of us will expect, especially when we first meet them. The thinking behind all of them is that the way we describe our behavior does fall into patterns and that these patterns give clues to our underlying personality. 'Clues' is the operative word. Not even a psychometrician would claim that a questionnaire could uncover the entire complexity of human personality, though they would claim that it could give strong hints.

Tips on filling in psychometric tests

■ Don't take too long. Your first answer is usually the best. These tests are not timed, but a candidate who takes double the average length of time may raise questions in the employer's mind about the speed at which they would normally work.

■ Look out for the social desirability questions. These are the ones which many tests include to check on how truthful you are being about yourself. For instance, there may be a question about white lies. You may think (correctly) that employers will not want to employ someone who is untruthful. However, everyone tells little white lies and to claim that you never do will raise doubts about whether you have filled in the rest of the test honestly.

■ Be honest. The best tests are very subtle in their construction and it is difficult to tell what factors they are assessing. Assume that there are no right answers and be yourself. Never try to second-guess what sort of personality type the employer may be looking for. The chances are you will be wrong, and even if you are right, you will not do yourself any favors by filling in the tests in a distorted way. You will only raise suspicions in the mind of the person who will be interpreting your results.

Group tasks

Here are some examples of group tasks set in Assessment Centers:

A. The group is given three large sheets of colored card, red, yellow, and blue, two pairs of scissors, a ruler, and some glue. The task is to make a toy which can be played with by the group at the end of the process. No other materials are allowed and the group has to complete its task in 40 minutes.
The underlying thinking here is:
This is a task where the resources are strictly limited and where cooperative behavior is essential to complete the task. It is also a task where there needs to be energy and creativity. It will help if there is some leadership. So this task is not unlike the sort of thing that many people have to do, i.e. produce something with limited resources in a short space of time with other people.
What is being tested:
Your resourcefulness, creativity, and your ability to cooperate with others.

B. The group is given a batch of papers which represent the papers being brought to one of the organization's committees. They are told that they are a working party meeting just this once to make a recommendation to the main committee on one of the topics in the papers. Time is allowed to read the papers – usually about half an hour.

Assessment centers

The underlying thinking here:
The ability to absorb complex information in a short time is essential in many organizations. Most issues on which such committees ponder are complex and cannot be reduced to simple yes/no answers. It is also essential to be able to work with people whose views may be dramatically different from your own, however irritating it may seem.

What is being tested:
Your patience, resilience, willingness to see an issue from many different sides, and the ability to press for a resolution.

C. Each person in the group is given a brief which represents a different point of view. The setting is often a contentious issue which needs to be resolved in a fictional organization. For instance, it may be that the setting is a merger between two organizations and the issue is what color should the vans of the new company be painted. You are not required to do any role-play in this exercise, only to represent the point of view on your brief.

The underlying thinking here:
Most organizations have issues where it is difficult to reconcile strongly held views. This type of meeting simulates meetings where these issues need to be thrashed out.

What is being tested:
Your ability to negotiate, willingness to listen to others, ability to put forward a view without alienating others, persuasiveness, and assertiveness.

Qualities

Usually, the person running the Center will tell you what qualities or behavior they are looking for. In any case this is no mystery – the qualities will relate directly to the skills that the employer has already told you (through the pre-interview paperwork) are needed.

Normally, the group task looks at how you interact with other people – are you bossy or helpful? Do you say too much or too little? Do you take the lead or wait for others? Do you listen?

Group tasks are designed on the principle that even in the stress of the assessment process, most of us will revert to type sooner or later, especially if our interest is gripped, and as nerves wear off, our true personality begins to emerge. My experience as a consultant certainly suggests that this is true.

As observer to this part of the selection process I have seen these examples among many others:

- The strongest candidate (on paper) showing undisguised irritation with other members of the group because of what he saw as their slowness to understand his point of view. The actual job involved working closely with committees drawn from various neighborhood organizations, so patience and ability to negotiate were paramount for the successful candidate. Another candidate was appointed on this occasion.

- Another strong candidate tried through a conscious use of silky charm to bring the group round to his way of thinking. When, however, that failed because they all ignored him, he turned to the observers as if to say, "What fools they all are," and, from that point on, took no further part in the discussion, leaning well back in his chair and folding his arms. He was not appointed.

- People, who have claimed to understand how to chair groups and run meetings, sitting dumbly and taking very little part in the process.

- An apparently weak candidate storming past the others through the sheer skill she showed in the group discussion by subtle chairing, charm, persuasiveness, and persistence. Her strong performance in the discussion forced the panel to look again at her CV and after an equally impressive interview she was offered the job.

- Two candidates having a head to head, violently conducted debate which excluded everyone else in the discussion – and no one else in the group attempting to remedy the situation. In this case, the panel did not appoint.

The striking thing about all these examples is that they were all for very senior jobs where skilled behavior in groups was a prerequisite of the posts, and all the candidates had claimed considerable experience in this area. Yet, alas, in four out of the five cases I cited here, the opposite seemed to be true on the evidence of the discussion.

The main point to remember here is that Assessment Centers are based on the idea that given long enough, or put under enough stress, most of us will give significant clues about our real selves. The aim is always to collect more data about you than is possible in an interview alone. So remember that everything you do is under observation. To do well in a Center you need to cultivate the idea of the inner observer who will ask you: "Is this how I really want to come across here?"

Behavior that helps at Assessment Centers

Learn the names of the other candidates during the day and make a point of using them during the discussion.

This is a basic courtesy and shows social skill. It will also make the other candidates listen to you – we all respond to hearing our names used.

Suggest in the first few minutes that the group spends a little time planning how you are going to have the discussion – for instance, should someone assume the formal role of facilitator/chair? How much time do you want to allocate to each aspect, should there be a period of brainstorming first?

Most groups of this sort plunge straight into the topic, without a thought for the planning aspect. A candidate who shows this kind of concern will always impress.

Enter into the discussion enthusiastically.

Enthusiasm is one of the main qualities that employers like and want; hanging back from taking part may look like shyness or diffidence.

However off the wall the other candidates' opinions seem to be, remain calm and patient.

It's only an exercise. Agitation that turns to irritation never helps in a negotiation.

Listen carefully to what the other candidates seem to be saying. Jot down main points on paper – briefly, just single words.

The majority of candidates do not do this – they quickly get into the ritual of queuing to speak – to get their own point across, regardless of what other people are saying.

Having listened, make the occasional brief summary of what other people have said, then put your views forward.

This is critically important behavior. First it shows that you have listened – otherwise you can't summarize properly. Secondly, it reassures the other members of the group that someone is keeping track of things. Research shows consistently that good negotiators listen about twice as often as they speak.

Explain the thinking behind your views, for instance by stating your assumptions explain how you got to a particular opinion.

Making your thinking visible in this way is rare. It is virtually always persuasive and shows both assertiveness and modesty.

Remind the group of how the time is going, by saying, for example: "We've been discussing this for ten minutes and we only have twenty minutes to get to a conclusion."

This is always a helpful behavior and again, shows you are taking responsibility for the group.

Identify common ground in the discussion – for instance: "Although we disagree on x, we all seem to agree on y, should we concentrate on that now?"

Many candidates mistakenly think that what is being assessed is their ability to trounce others by talking them down and dominating the group. This is rarely what is being assessed. On the contrary, the panel is normally looking for someone with excellent interpersonal skills who can find a path through the thickets of misunderstanding that can occur in any discussion or meeting. Identifying and drawing attention to common ground is the valued behavior here.

Make "process" observations. In other words, draw attention to the process in which the group is involved rather than just its task. For instance, say things like: "I notice that every time we touch on topic x, we all start talking across each other…"

The majority of candidates in this kind of exercise get completely absorbed in the task and forget the process, yet neglecting the process is one of the main ways in which this kind of discussion goes wrong in the "real" world. Observers seeing a candidate who is able to make process observations are usually impressed.

As you get near the end of the discussion, summarize all the main points that have been made and invite the group to draw conclusions.

This shows concern for closure – a useful leadership behavior.

Giving a presentation

Another common technique is to ask you to make an individual presentation, sometimes to a wider group than the normal panel; for instance, when senior staff positions in local government are being filled, city councillors are sometimes invited to be present for this part of the selection process. The topic is normally what your strategy would be if you got the job. For example, if the job is a senior one to head up a unit, then you may be asked to outline how you would deal with staff, the unit's clients, its systems, policies, training, and so on.

What is being tested here is your self-presentation:

Do you have a big presence or are you timid?
Can you hold the interest of an audience?
Are you articulate?
Do you know how to explain complex issues simply and vividly?
For any job where persuasiveness is one of the competencies, a presentation can be a useful pointer to your level of skill. Practice, coaching, and feedback can improve your performance enormously.

You will normally be given advance notice of the topic and will be able to prepare the content in advance. Sometimes, you will only be told the topic on the day and will be given a limited amount of time for preparation. It would be very unusual to be given no notice and no time, though that, too, can happen occasionally.

Preparing the content

Think first about your audience. What can you assume they already know? What are their likely interests and concerns? If you were sitting in their place, what would you be interested and impressed to hear?

Now think about the points you want to make. You may be given anything from 5 to 15 minutes to make your presentation. However much time you have, bear in mind the three-point rule. This is the one that says that the human mind cannot retain any more than three points from a verbal presentation. This is a sensible rule of thumb. These three points should be the spine of what you are going to say.

Early on in your presentation, build in a reminder of your authority and credibility. For instance, if what you are going to talk about is your plan for what could (if you got the job) become your department, remind the audience of your experience and credentials in your field.

It is also useful to build in a clear verbal structure to what you are going to say. This helps you to make yourself clear, and it also helps the audience to see where you are going.

So, for instance, you could say something like: *"I'm going to talk about three things here, x, y, and z topics. First, x…"*(then you talk about x).

"Now I'm going to go on to y topic…" (then you talk about y).

"And finally, I'm going to say a little about z…" (then you talk about z).

Then you summarize: *"So in this presentation I've talked about three things, x, y, and z and my conclusion is that…"* (you give your conclusion).

This follows the advice of "first you tell them what you're going to tell them, then you tell them, then you tell them what you've told them."

Your first few words

It's no accident that television and radio producers devote so much time, skill and energy to working out how the first few seconds of a program should have maximum impact. In fact, pro rata, some very simple TV programs have more money and time spent on their opening graphics than go into the program itself. This is because people decide within a few seconds whether or not to hit that remote control button and change channels. Your audience can't do that, but they can "switch off" their intellect unless you grab their attention straight away.

This kind of presentation is probably not the place for a joke, unless you can tell it very well.

Some good ideas for these opening moments include:

A personal anecdote (the safest).
A startling statistic.
A quotation.
A challenging statement.

It is worth learning your opening sentence – this can carry you over the dreaded moment of actually starting to speak. It's never a good idea to read or try to learn the rest of your presentation. It inevitably comes across as stilted and conveys a lack of confidence. A presentation is not a lecture or a sermon.

If you want the confidence of writing out the whole thing first, do so, especially to time yourself, but then reduce it to a few index cards if you want the assurance of not drying up. Cards are better than large pieces of paper because they are less obtrusive. Choose large cards and write no more than few key words on each in big letters that can be read at a glance. Highlight them as well, if you think that will help.

One additional tip: punch a hole in the corner of each card then run a thread, split ring or treasury tag through them so that they stay in the right order as you turn them over. Nervousness may cause you to drop the cards – this way, they won't scatter everywhere.

Giving a presentation

As an alternative, if you know that there will be an overhead projector available and you are confident in its use, prepare overhead transparencies. These do away with the need for additional notes and also give your audience something to look at other than you. This can be useful as the thing many presenters most dread is the feeling of so many pairs of eyes gazing at them.

With OHPs, keep the content to no more than five lines in large, bold, lower-case type – for instance 20 point. Lower case is much easier to read than capitals. Even more professionally, if you are familiar with Powerpoint, and the equipment is available, you can use that, but you need to be certain that there will be no technical glitches.

Some candidates have impressed panels and appointing committees by bringing along handouts of the main points of their presentations. This is probably a good idea, though it will be worth checking out with the panel chairperson first. If you do decide to take this path, double check for typos, and take care with design and layout. It is unlikely that the panel will want to read anything too long – a page or two at most is likely to be the limit of their interest.

Checklist on content	Yes	Your notes
1. Have you identified what your audience's needs are?		
2. What three points are you going to make to them?		
3. How will you open your presentation?		
4. Have you reduced the content to index cards?		
5. If you want to use an OHP or Powerpoint, is the equipment available?		

Preparing yourself

However wonderful the content, you will impress even more if you convey confidence and authority in how you speak and somehow communicate that you are in touch with the audience and care how they react to you.

Long after we have forgotten the content of what even the most informative speaker has said, we may be able to remember how he or she spoke.

Conveying confidence and authority

This is done in two ways: how you use your body and how you use your voice.

Always stand; never ever try to do a presentation sitting down. Standing when your audience is sitting immediately gives you a height advantage. Stand with your body in a graceful straight line with your feet planted slightly apart. Keep your shoulders down – this conveys relaxation. Don't turn one knee out or lean away with your shoulder or cock your head to one side. These (and other variants of the same thing) convey uncertainty.

Keep your hands lightly together, holding your cards, or if you can do it without notes, just leave your arms dangling loosely at your side. Don't have your hands in your pockets or clasped in front of you, nor in a "steepling" shape which may look as if you are praying for divine help.

Another good tip is to avoid waving your arms about too much or keeping them too rigidly at your sides. Either of these extremes, again, conveys lack of authority.

You should mentally stake out your space and occupy it while giving the presentation. This means that you should take a few steps back, forward, and sideways while you are speaking. If you remain rooted to the spot, you may unwittingly convey the "tethered elephant" look, and seem as if you lack confidence. If you overdo it (unlikely in the stress of the presentation) and roam about too much, you will look like a caged lion and become distracting to your audience.

People who have fine tuned the art of this technique use the moment of moving to emphasize a point – in other words they capture the audience's attention through movement and then give their punchlines.

Your voice is very important. Check if everyone can hear you before you get going. Keep your volume up and vary the tone. Remember that it is fine to use pauses and emphasis. There is special value in pausing for two or three seconds before you start the presentation – that is at the moment when you are sure that you have everyone's attention. This shows confidence and also gives you a moment to collect your thoughts.

Keeping in touch with the audience

It can feel scary or exhilarating to be the focus of so many eyes. However, the most important point here is to remember to use the so-called lighthouse effect. This means constantly sweeping the group with eye contact. Look out for the way politicians do this to very large audiences. They slowly rake the room, giving people the impression that they are personally communicating with each and every person there. It's much easier, of course, with a smaller group. There, you really can make brief (a second or so) eye contact with each person before moving steadily on to the person sitting next to them and then back the other way.

The reason for this is that without eye contact, we lose interest in what someone is saying. Also, it gives you immediate feedback. Is the audience looking interested, bored, fidgety, entranced? Are they really listening to you? It's only by keeping the eye contact going that you will know the answer, enabling you to modify the length and content of your presentation as you go.

This simple rule of communication is the one I see broken most often. For instance, I see people whose content and voice is excellent, but who:

- Address only one side of the room.
- Persistently miss out the people sitting at the extreme edge of the group.
- Talk to the ceiling.
- Talk to the flip chart, projector, or their notes.
- Talk to the tops of people's chairs.
- Talk to the spaces between people's chairs.

The other simple rule to remember is to SMILE. If you look too serious it will be off-putting. Smiling conveys that you are comfortable with what you want to say and hope that others are also enjoying it.

Warm-ups

Giving a presentation is a kind of audition. The part you are acting is yourself, and the role you are auditioning for is Best Candidate. No actor would dream of going on stage without some kind of physical warm up. The suggestions which follow come from acting training – and they do really work.

Repeat the breathing exercise described on p. 30. If your breathing is shallow, it will be impossible to project your voice. Correct breathing also helps you feel relaxed.

Now shake your arms for a few moments, then do the same with each leg. This warms up the muscles and helps lose tension. Flop your body downwards so that your arms just dangle loosely in front of you. Now slowly and gracefully stand up sweeping your arms above your head and around to the side in an arc, ending with your arms at your side again. Do this four or five times.

Finally, don't be afraid to show some passion. I once coached a manager who was concerned about his presentation style. When talking about relationships with suppliers in a practice presentation he was satisfactory, but his heart did not seem to be in it and he was less persuasive than he could have been. I asked him to talk to me instead about his favorite baseball team, a subject I already knew he really cared about. The difference was startling. He came alive, was funny, compelling and fluent. The challenge for him was to talk about his suppliers with this same enthusiasm.

Without passion and its close companions, sincerity, and authenticity, it is hard to persuade people to listen to you. Show passion through speaking eagerly. Don't be afraid to let it show.

You are going to be doing a lot of communicating with your face, so it is important to get the facial muscles warmed up too. Three exercises help here:

- **Chewing sticky toffee: imagine you have a mouth full of really sticky toffee that you are chewing. This gets the muscles of your mouth warmed up. Do this for about a minute.**

- **Sticking your tongue vigorously in and out, in and out for about a minute. Feeling tongue-tied is a handicap that bedevils many presenters. This exercise helps get around the problem by getting the tongue used to working.**

- **Massaging your face with your hands. Work around the face with both hands, massaging gently so that the whole face feels loosened up.**

'Trial by orange juice'

The Assessment Center will often offer you the chance to meet a group of staff, usually over a buffet lunch. If it is a very senior appointment, there may be members of the board present. In making appointments to a charitable foundation, for instance, it would be common for trustees to attend at this point. There may also be more junior people present.

The purpose of the lunch is three-fold. One is to assess you and how you behave with your potential colleagues. Another is to help you decide whether or not you want to belong to the company and the third is to give you the chance to inform yourself about the organization and its issues. It may be a very useful source of information for any points which you want to raise in your panel interview.

What to do

Remember that you are under close observation. The people who attend the lunch will be asked informally for their views of you, even if they do not have a vote in making the final selection.

■ Circulate – make sure you talk to everyone, this is not the time for social shyness. Smile, introduce yourself and ask what the other person's role is in the organization.

■ Be prepared to give a mini-biography about yourself. People will be curious about you and how you have got to where you are and what draws you to the job. Don't go on too long – a few minutes is enough.

■ Ask questions about what the issues are as the other person sees them. Listen carefully and show that you are listening by skillful summarizing. Beware of appearing to interrogate – keep it light, it's a social occasion as well as an assessment. Don't exclude other candidates, who if they have any sense, will be doing the same.

■ Share the conversation.

■ If there are junior staff present, treat these individuals graciously. They are a valuable source of information about the job and the organization but remember they will also be reporting back on you. This will apply even if they would be more junior than you if you got the job.

A better experience

A well-designed Assessment Center can actually be an exhilarating and enjoyable process. It is taxing, certainly, but its very thoroughness is reassuring. It feels much fairer than a stand-alone panel interview because you have had more chance to show what you can do. It puts internal and external candidates on much more of an equal footing and is much more likely to identify the strongest candidate.

Altogether, Assessment Centers have one purpose and one purpose only: to increase the amount of data available to the employer about each candidate. After a properly run center, the employer is much better informed about:

- Your intellectual capacity.
- Your aptitude for the job.
- Your personality.
- How you behave with other people.
- How you behave under stress.
- How you behave when more relaxed.
- How far what you have claimed about yourself is borne out by what you have done during the Center.
- Whether you really want the job.

Note: if you encounter an Assessment Center you should expect the following as good ethical practice:

- The purpose of every activity clearly explained.
- Clear instructions.
- The offer of proper feedback on all tests.
- Being given your test results to take away.
- No selection decision ever being based on the result of any one test.
- Due regard being paid to the way nervousness could affect your performance.

The practice interview

You will enormously increase your chances of getting the job if you have a practice interview. This is because the practice is like a good dress-rehearsal for a play – it's the place to spot the flaws and sort them out before the performance. It gets you fluent in talking about the job and your approach to it. It helps deal with nerves because you will have the confidence that practice gives. Also, if you choose your practice – interviewer carefully, you will receive invaluable feedback on how you come across.

The ideal practice-interviewer is a sympathetic mentor – someone perhaps a little older or more experienced who is friendly, patient, cares about your career, but is not too emotionally involved with you.

This will make it easier for you to hear his or her advice. The practice interviewer does not need to know anything about the job. If you can't identify someone like this, then a friend, colleague, parent, or partner can also do a good job. It is better to have even a rough-and-ready practice than none.

How to do the practice interview

- Set aside at least an hour where you can guarantee not to be interrupted.
- Brief your interviewer about the job, giving them any paperwork about it.
- Give them a copy of your application.
- Suggest some general areas for questions without giving them an actual script.
- Run the practice as if it was real – never mind if it seems embarrassing or silly, just press on.
- Ask your interviewer to take notes on how you come across.
- Devote at least 20 minutes to discussing their feedback on how you did.
- Leave time to have a second attempt at any wobbly areas revealed by the practice.

When you have run the interview, give your interviewer this check list and go through it together.

Did I	Excellently	OK	Area for attention
Smile?			
Convey confidence?			
Sit up, looking relaxed and alert throughout the interview?			
Remain courteous and friendly, even when probed or put under pressure?			
Keep replies to 2-3 minutes?			
Speak clearly and audibly?			
Keep my language simple and direct?			
Use direct experience to illustrate my answers?			
Maintain appropriate eye contact?			
Show enthusiasm for the tasks the job would involve?			
Show that I understand the organization and its issues?			

Inevitably there will be some weak areas and some strong ones. If you and your helper have the time, it will pay great dividends to re-visit the weaker areas. One rehearsal is probably enough. More than one may make you seem a little over-rehearsed, and also raises the danger that you will get too fixed in your answers, so when the real interviewers ask their questions it takes you by surprise that they are not the same as the ones you practiced.

4

If you don't get the job
Negotiating terms
Starting the new job

Getting feedback

Do I really want the job?

Understanding change

If you don't get the job

Most employers understand how anxious candidates are to hear the result of the interview. It is good practice to let everyone know the outcome the same day, or at the very latest the next day. This should include an explanation for any delays that may be occurring. When this doesn't happen and you are still left in limbo, you can make any of the following assumptions:

- The panel can't agree and will have to meet again.
- The panel are not enthusiastic about any of the candidates they have seen and are going to return to their original list of applicants without closing down their options on their existing shortlist.
- Another candidate has been offered the job but is holding out for better terms.
- The person delegated to tell everyone is too busy to make this a priority.
- This is a boorish group of people and can't be bothered to let you know that you were not successful.

The more time goes on without contact, the less likely it is that you are the successful candidate. However, if you still haven't heard after three days, you should call the panel chairperson and ask what is happening, expressing your continuing interest in the post. Most probably you will be told that you have not gotten the job. If so, follow the advice in the next section.

Ask for feedback

A conscientious employer will offer this routinely, but mostly this is a duty that interviewers hate. Nobody enjoys giving bad news and many interviewers have never had any training in how to give feedback. It's just as hard to hear bad news, so it takes courage to ask, but ask you must. This is particularly important if you are getting plenty of interviews but are not getting the jobs as there may be something about your interview technique that is getting in the way.

How to do it

- By telephone – this is not a process which can be done by letter.
- Say how sorry you were not to get the job but don't make a big deal of it – the employer does not want to be made to feel guilty.
- Say: *"I'm interested in your feedback on the quality of my application. What, specifically would help me be a stronger candidate next time."* (Or, *"Is there some further experience I should specifically get?"*).
- Now ask about the interview itself. Say something like: *"Could you give me some feedback on how I came across at the interview?"* or, *"What do you think would help me be more effective another time?"*
- If you get evasive replies, such as: *"Well, you were a bit quiet"*, press the point by saying: *"Could you give me an example?"*
- Where you get vague replies, press for clarification. For instance, if the reply is something like: *"Well you seemed rather lost at that point in the interview"*, then say: *"Could you tell me what it was about what I said or did that made me seem lost?"*

When you have heard the points people make, take the time to summarize them. This has two purposes. First, it ensures that you really have heard the points that have been made. Secondly, it makes a good impression on the other person because it shows that you have got the courage to say out loud whatever critical things have been said about you or your record.

- Don't under any circumstances get defensive. Don't answer back or argue. Most especially, don't give excuses such as: *"Well I had a cold that day,"* or *"My husband was in hospital so I couldn't concentrate."* However genuine the reasons for what you feel was a poorer performance than normal, the interviewer will not want to hear it, and it will sound like an excuse. Listen carefully to make sure you've understood the feedback.
- Thank the other person enthusiastically for their time.
- Remember feedback is just feedback. It's not an instruction to change, though most feedback, even when it is clumsily given, has some truth in it from which we can learn something useful.

An exceptionally well-qualified senior manager was persistently failing at interviews. He asked me for help. My first suggestion was to encourage him to ask for feedback from panels he had recently attended. In spite of meeting considerable embarrassment, he persisted, using the techniques described on this page. The message was clear. To his utter amazement, he was told that he was conveying "arrogance." Working on his interview technique so that he conveyed more humility ensured that he did get the next job that came up.

The follow-up letter

If you do get the job

You should still ask for feedback, and if appropriate, you should still write a thank-you letter to the panel chairperson.

A neglected tool

A few years ago I was chairing a panel to appoint an occupational psychologist. There were two strong candidates and one was duly offered, and accepted, the job. The other wrote a very charming letter of thanks for the opportunity to attend the interview, saying how much he had enjoyed it. As a result, although he hadn't got the job, he did get two lucrative assignments as a freelance consultant!

The follow-up letter is a severely neglected tool by virtually all job-seekers. In my experience, I can only think of a handful who bothered to do it. In every case it earned them a useful advantage.

Some examples:

- One got offered the next vacancy without having to go through another interview.
- One got offered a temporary stint as a trainee.
- One was recommended to another employer.
- One was invited back for some free career counselling.

Your ego may feel bruised because you didn't get the job. You may feel the last thing you want is any further contact with the panel. You may feel you gave a poor account of yourself.

No matter, write that letter:

- It's a further chance to demonstrate initiative.
- It gives you another shot at reminding the employer who you are.
- It's courteous and shows a proper concern for the people-side of life.

In the letter, the format should be:

Opening paragraph thanks them for the chance to be interviewed and says you were naturally disappointed not to be offered the job.

Second paragraph emphasizes your experience and maybe has something on any misleading impression you think you may have given during the interview itself.

Third paragraph conveys your continuing interest in the organization and asks them to bear you in mind for future vacancies.

Negotiating Terms

However brilliantly things appear to be going, never negotiate salary during the interview:

- You are in a weak position because you have not been offered the job.
- The tension and excitement of the interview is not the right frame of mind in which to negotiate.
- Entering a negotiation makes it seem as if you are agreeing that you want the job when actually it is too soon to say – you need time to consider such an important decision calmly.

The time to negotiate is when you have been made a definite offer and when you are clear that you want to say yes. It is unlikely that either of these conditions will be satisfied at the interview itself.

Fending off salary negotiations during the interview

A trained interviewer will not press you about you salary expectations, but an untrained one may. His or her questions may include:

- What salary are you looking for?
- What if we can't match what you're earning now?
- Would you expect a car with this job?

Your reply should be a courteous, friendly one along the lines of: *"If we both agree that I'm the best person for this job, I'd rather talk about salary then."* If the interviewer insists on a reply, then you need to have an answer prepared (see later). However, again, a safer answer is to say: *"I'm looking for something in the range of $X,000–$Y,000, depending on how the package is made up."*

Just as the interview itself is too early for the negotiation, it is also possible to leave the negotiation too late. Too late is when you have actually formally accepted the job. Much too late is when you have started the job. By then you have lost all your bargaining power.

Do I really want the job?

A surprising number of people experience a panic of indecision at this point. They do a successful interview and are offered the job. But now that the flirtation stage has passed and marriage is about to be proposed, they are not so sure. Do I really want to uproot my family and go to live in another city? It's an interesting job all right, but the salary is less than I'd hoped for. I'm not sure I want to identify myself with that organization – and so on.

The agonizing uncertainty may be made a lot worse if your old employer, getting wind of the offer, suddenly offers you a blank check to stay. All of this may be made worse again if the process of going through the interview has raised doubts about how attractive the job really is.

It is useful to do a prioritizing exercise at this point, to sort out in your own mind what you really want from work.

Step 1

Fill in the dark blue boxes down the right-hand side of the chart first by answering these questions: what do you most enjoy about your present job or, if you prefer, what is most important to you in any job? Examples might be: "the chance to travel;" "the opportunity to organise my own work"; "direct contact with x or y kind of person;" and so on. Just write down your answers in any order.

Step 2

In the grids on the left, compare item 1 with item 2, circling whichever is most important to you, then continue down the grid, comparing item 1 with item 3, item 2 with item 3 and so on until you have got to the end of the grid.

Step 3

Fill in the table below, looking back on your grid to see how many times you ringed each item. On the final line, write the order in which you have ranked each item.

Items for prioritising in any order

1									
1 / 2	2								
1 / 3	2 / 3	3							
1 / 4	2 / 4	3 / 4	4						
1 / 5	2 / 5	3 / 5	4 / 5	5					
1 / 6	2 / 6	3 / 6	4 / 6	5 / 6	6				
1 / 7	2 / 7	3 / 7	4 / 7	5 / 7	6 / 7	7			
1 / 8	2 / 8	3 / 8	4 / 8	5 / 8	6 / 8	7 / 8	8		
1 / 9	2 / 9	3 / 9	4 / 9	5 / 9	6 / 9	7 / 9	8 / 9	9	
1 / 10	2 / 10	3 / 10	4 / 10	5 / 10	6 / 10	7 / 10	8 / 10	9 / 10	10

1	2	3	4	5	6	7	8	9	10	Item number
										How many times did you ring that item?
										Final ranking

Do I really want the job?

Step 4.

Now write out your list of priorities in the final order. This should give you some robust guidance on what you want and need in any new job.

Step 5

Now stack the potential new job against the old one to provide a comparative list. Give a tick for each point that either job earns.

Your priorities	Old job	New job
1		
2		
3		
4		
5		
6		
7		
8		
9		
10		
	Total	

If you are still undecided after this exercise, ask yourself what your reservations are, and write them down or talk them through with a friend or partner. Typically, the questions still nagging away at this point are to do with unknowns in the new job. How much autonomy will I have? Do I really like this boss? Can I really do this job? Do I really want all the upheaval of the change?

Now ask yourself these questions

- On a scale of 1 to 10, how much do these reservations matter?
- What further information could help resolve them?
- Where can I obtain this information?

If your decision is "no," then let the employer know immediately so that they can re-assemble the panel and consider what to do. There may be another good candidate who is still waiting to hear. If it's "yes" then get into negotiating the salary immediately.

Preparing for the negotiation

Where the job has been advertised, a salary or salary range may have been quoted. This may still leave room for flexibility on either side, though there may be less than you think. For instance, if you are young and inexperienced in the employer's eye, he or she may try to negotiate downwards. If the employer knows that you are already earning above the ceiling quoted, he or she may expect to pay a little over the odds. In hierarchical or highly bureaucratic organizations there may be rigid rules, particularly about entry-point jobs.

The best deal is going to be the one which leaves both sides feeling satisfied – neither side feeling sore, resentful, or triumphant. You have to work together and you do not want the relationship tainted from the start.

You will need to make a realistic assessment of the power balance on both sides. If your offer came quickly and the employer is clearly eager to take you on, you can probably safely assume that you have considerable bargaining power. If the reverse is true – the offer came perhaps because another candidate dropped out, or if there is a perfectly respectable internal candidate waiting in the wings, then you are on thinner ground and may have to be more modest in what you ask for.

Do I really want the job?

Your own research

First, be clear what your salary needs are. How much do you need after taxes to meet your obligations and your other needs? It is worth doing some careful calculations here – the total may be a lot less or a lot more than you think.

Next, find out what the going rate for the job is. What did your predecessor, if there was one, earn? What do people in similar jobs in this or other organizations earn? Look in the job ads in the papers to check out your impressions if necessary.

Finally, think carefully about the value of so-called "fringe" benefits. Many are not such a "fringe" and may be worth more than you think; for instance, some employers make very generous contributions to 401k pension plans or underwrite health insurance programs. But some employee benefits may be worth less than they seem. A company car, for example, can be a dubious "perk" if by giving it the employer justifies paying you less in salary – especially if the car is classified as income for purposes of federal income tax. You might be better off using your own car on company business, particularly if the company offers a generous mileage rate.

Similarly, signing a fixed-term contract as an independent contractor may gain you a somewhat higher basic rate, but if you have to fund your own pension plan and pay your own health insurance costs and cede all your legal rights as a full-time employee, it may not be quite so attractive a proposition without much greater compensation.

It helps during the actual negotiation to find out – perhaps by asking directly – how much room for manoeuver there is. Some employers honestly cannot go above a stated ceiling; others may have a wide range in mind.

Many employers are wary of hiring at the top of the range, especially if they feel you are still a relatively unknown quantity. Where this is the case, it is often possible to negotiate a salary review say, six months into the job, where if you are as good as you claim, you and your boss will sit down and re-negotiate your salary.

This and other details needs to be built into your contract of employment – a legal entitlement. The contract need not be a "legalistic" document – a letter is fine, but it does need to state:

■ Salary.
■ Notice period on either side.
■ Pension position.
■ Fringe benefits.
■ Hours, even if there are no set hours.
■ Holiday and vacation entitlement.
■ Duties.
■ How performance will be judged.

Starting the job

When you start your new job, there is usually a period of disillusionment on both sides. You may feel overwhelmed with the stress of learning a new job and a new organization and getting to know a lot of new people all at once. You may experience a sudden loss of self-esteem as the difficulties of the work become apparent. You may feel lonely because there is no one who feels like a friend.

You may find out that there are all sorts of niggling little details which remind you of what you have lost by moving jobs – especially if you were laid off from your previous job and you are now earning a smaller salary. You may, for instance, catch yourself thinking sentimentally about apparently trivial things like the scruffy old cafeteria at your former place of work. It takes effort to get to know new colleagues and to find out what the job is really about when all the excitement of the selection process is over.

On the boss's side, there is often a parallel process of disappointment. The boss discovers that you are not the perfect candidate after all because you are only human. If you take advantage of the advice offered below, you can short circuit the process of disillusionment on both sides. Your task in the first few weeks is NOT to do the new job, it's to learn how to do it – a rather different emphasis. Remember that there was a process of mutual choosing which led to the offer and acceptance of a job, and that this probably means it is the right job for you. If it isn't, then it's not a life sentence and you can move on. Much more likely, you are going through a normal process of adjustment and will learn to do – and love – the job.

It is sensible in the first few weeks of a new job to

- Come to work early.
- Show eagerness, initiative, and willingness to learn.
- Schedule a session with your boss to explore what he or she expects from you in the first month and the five months after that.
- Introduce yourself to team members and make sure you have a meal or a drink with some of them in the first week.
- Ask team members what the do's and don'ts are of working in the organization – for instance, what customs are there which everyone knows but which no one explains unless you ask? What time do people start and finish work?

Starting the job

- Make sure that if there are other people doing the same job as you, you talk to the outstanding performers (ask who they are, everyone will know) and ask them what advice they would give you about how to succeed within the organization.
- Avail yourself of any new employee training programs that may be offered by the organization.
- Ask people to explain any unfamiliar jargon and anything else you don't understand.
- Get to see the core business of the organization in action: for instance, if it makes widgets, visit the place where the widgets are made. It doesn't matter if your own job is not directly connected with widget-making; you still need to know everything you can about widgets because the most important people in the organization will probably have a passion for widgets and you need to know why.
- Make sure you limit your references to how you did things at your old organization: it can be irritating to others because it suggests that you think your old way was superior.

Have I made a mistake here?

When you still feel desperately at sea with a new job, even after availing yourself of all the ideas listed above, then of course it is possible that you really have made a mistake, and so has the employer. If so, you have a number of options.

One is to stick it out for a reasonable period of time and then to start the search for a new job. This probably means committing yourself to at least 18 months in the job. Another option is just to wait and see – you may be wrong and with time, you could settle in to the job. The third option is to get out of the job as quickly as possible. A swift exit is probably the easiest to explain to any future employer. Of course, if you do this, it leaves you without a job, and taking this path will depend on how desperate you are to have a job. You may be able to freelance while looking for another job or it may even be possible to go back to the job you have just left.

Whatever you decide to do it is essential to talk it through carefully with your boss. Sometimes in all the stress of starting a new job it is possible to get things out of proportion.

Understanding personal change

Mostly, such drastic action is rarely needed and you will settle well into the new job. However, a change of job is a major life-shift and like all such changes, the psychological adjustment can take time. In one well-known list of stressors, changing jobs comes high up for potential to cause disturbance and misery, along with the death of a loved one, moving your residence and getting divorced. This is in spite of the fact that the change is one that you probably initiated and wanted. If the change was forced on you through the process of being laid off or fired, then the potential for feeling disturbed and upset is clearly much higher.

Letting go

Even a wanted change involves some loss. It will help if you have been able to "mourn" the passing of the old job; for instance if you have had a proper farewell party with speeches and presents. This makes it clear to you and to everyone else that something has really ended, just as a funeral makes it clear that a life is really over. It's probably better to cut your ties with the old job, avoiding going back to the building, and only keeping contact with the people who genuinely became your friends.

Using the transition period wisely

It is useful to have a consciously planned period of transition between the old job and the new, even if it only a few days of "hanging loose" and doing nothing at home between ending the old job and starting the new. Even better may be to have a short vacation, if you have the time and money. However long or short this time is, use it to refresh, to think, to take stock – for instance of your skills and where they may need to be refreshed. See friends, read, walk, go to a movie – whatever delights you and helps you enjoy the feeling of making the journey from one way of earning a living to another.

Committing to the new

Similarly, it helps if your new boss has been thoughtful enough to arrange a welcome party for you, or some kind of semi-formal professional and social occasion which accelerates the process of bonding with your new colleagues.

It also helps to make a point of finding one or two confidants, people who can share the funny little ways of the organization with you and help you understand its culture.

Finally, this whole process of adjustment can be speeded up considerably by throwing yourself wholeheartedly into new projects which have your signature on them and which you can shape.

In any process of personal change, it can help to remember that the actual change and the psychological adjustment may be two separate things. You can end the old job but still feel attached to it. You can start the new job on the agreed upon date, but the real process of adaptation is a much slower process.
You can hurry it up to some extent by using the ideas on this page, but some of it will just take time. Let this happen and allow for the natural process of adjustment to take place.

Index

Answers, 42-43
  model, 52
  to awkward questions, 57
Asking questions, 58
Assessment centres, 62-77
  timed ability tests, 62
  timed aptitude tests, 62
  psychometric tests, 62-65
  in-tray exercises, 62
  group tasks, 65-66
Awkward questions, 55-57
Balance of power, 37
Body language, 41
Breathing, 30
Competency analysis, 21
Confirmation, 34
"Customer focus", 21
Double questions, 49
Dressing for interviews, 28
Evidence-based technique, 44-45
Executive search, 38
Fears, 36
Feedback, 82-83
Follow-up letter, 84
"Funnelling down", 45
Getting there, 35
"Givers", 43
Group tasks, 35
Head-hunting, 38
Hypothetical questions, 50
Interviewer, 14
  incompetent, 49-54
In-tray exercises, 62
Job description, 9-10, 21

Leading questions, 54
Lying, 46
matching, 41
Mental rehearsal, 31
Model answers, 52
Negotiating terms, 85, 89, 90
nerves, 30
Off-the-wall questions, 53
On-the-spot hire, 60-61
Panel, 15
Person specification, 21
Politically incorrect questions, 51
Practice interview, 78-79
Presentations
  audience, 74
  conveying confidence, 73
  giving, 70-73
  preparation, 73
  warm-up, 74
Psychometric tests, 62-65
Questions, 42-43
  asking, 58
  awkward, 55
  double, 49
  hypothetical, 50
  leading, 54
  off-the-wall, 53
  politically incorrect, 51
  rambling, 49
  triple, 49
Rambling questions, 49
Rapport, 40-41
Research, 18-23
Salary, negotiating, 46

Selection, 11
Self-presentation, 28-29
Social skills, 39-41
Starting the job, 91-93
"Takers", 43
Timed ability tests, 63
Timed aptitude tests, 63
Triple questions, 49
Unfriendly practices, 61
USP, 24-27
Visualizing, 30
Voice, 41

If you liked Effective Interviews check out these career-building books from AMACOM.

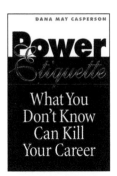

Power Etiquette
What You Don't Know Can Kill Your Career
Dana May Casperson

Power Etiquette tells you all the things you need to know about business etiquette. It covers a wide range of subjects, and it includes valuable information on such timely topics such as "netiquette" (internet and e-mail etiquette), cell phone dos and don'ts, and video and teleconferencing manners.
$14.95 ISBN: 0-8144-7998-7

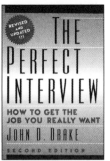

The Perfect Interview
John Drake

This exceptionally useful guide is packed with expert advice on how to ace that interview— and get the offer you deserve. The new edition also supplies answers to twenty of the toughest questions interviewers ask, real-life stories of both good and bad interviewing situations, suggestions on preparing psychologically for the interview, and more!
$17.95 ISBN: 0-8144-7919-7

Personal Magnetism
Discover Your Own Charisma and Learn to Charm, Inspire, and Influence Others
Andrew J. DuBrin

Personal Magnetism will teach you to improve charismatic traits such as humanism, optimism, enthusiasm, and self-confidence, strengthen your relationships, learn from charismatic leaders, turn criticism into positive suggestions, use extraverbal communication and humor to exude magnetism, and more.
$17.95 ISBN: 0-8144-7936-7

Career Bounce-Back!
The Professionals In Transition™ Guide to Recovery & Reemployment
J. Damian Birkel With Stacey J. Miller

"Here's the ultimate survival guide to unemployment. It tells you not only how to get another job fast, but also how to get a better one that improves your life spiritually, professionally, and financially."
—*Thomas O'Neil, Editorial Director, Hearst Magazines Enterprises*
$14.95 ISBN 0-8144-7954-5

Call 1-800-262-9699 or order in your local bookstore.